# Adirondack Cookbook

# Adirondack Cookbook

Hallie E. Bond and Stephen Topper

**GIBBS SMITH**
TO ENRICH AND INSPIRE HUMANKIND

*For Meg, Alex, and Mason, with love and thanks for your*
*good nature in sampling the results of my research—*
*from "dog-chokers" to spruce beer.*    —H. B.

*I dedicate this work to the mountains, forests, lakes, and streams*
*of the Adirondacks that have not only provided fine fare for*
*the table, but also the fresh air to clear my mind.*    —ST

First Edition
18 17 16 15 14      5 4 3 2 1

Text © 2014 Hallie E. Bond and
Stephen Topper

Images courtesy of the Adirondack
Museum

Published by
Gibbs Smith
P.O. Box 667
Layton, Utah 84041

1.800.835.4993 orders
www.gibbs-smith.com

Designed by Michelle Farinella Design

Printed and bound in Korea

Gibbs Smith books are printed on
either recycled, 100% post-consumer
waste, FSC-certified papers or on
paper produced from sustainable
PEFC-certified forest/controlled wood
source. Learn more at www.pefc.org.

Library of Congress Cataloging-in-
Publication Data

Bond, Hallie E.
  Adirondack cooking / Hallie Bond
and Stephen Topper. — First edition.
    pages cm
  Includes index.
  ISBN 978-1-4236-3273-3
  1. Cooking—New York (State)—
Adirondack Mountains. 2. Cooking,
American. I. Topper, Stephen. II. Title.
  TX715.B696 2014
  641.5973—dc23
                        2013029267

# Contents

# Introduction

*Foodies talk a lot about* terroir *these days.* The term originally was used to describe how wine tastes of the land where the grapes were grown, but now it's being applied to all kinds of agricultural products. Terroir usually takes in natural conditions like climate and soils. In this book, we are broadening the concept to mean the cultural climate of whole dishes. The following pages contain recipes to please the modern palate that were inspired by the foods and foodways of the Adirondack past.

A vast state park enclosing most of northern New York north of the Mohawk River encompasses the Adirondack Mountains today. The six million acres of this reserve seem like a wilderness to modern-day visitors. The only interstate highway skirts the very edge of the park and most roads are two-lane, winding corridors through tunnels of trees. The landscape is covered with deep forests, lakes, streams, and rivers. But there have been people in the Adirondacks for thousands of years and, of course, they had to eat.

From time immemorial, the Mohawk came into the mountains from their homes to the south and the Western Abenaki from their territories to the west. They brought with them their staple foods of corn, beans, and squash, and feasted on wild foods they found here, both animal and vegetable. Yankee loggers, miners, and a few intrepid farmers began moving into the region after the American Revolution, and by 1845 visitors to places like Long Lake, in the center of the mountains, reported clusters of log houses and cleared fields scattered along the lakeshores. In these fields, the settlers grew crops like buckwheat, oats, and rye, which were suited to the cool, damp climate, and they adopted the crops of the Indians. As they had in New England, the settlers kept pigs and perhaps a cow, but they, like the Indians, hunted and gathered the bounty of the woods in order to survive. Irish immigrants and French-speaking Québeçois settled the mountains in the nineteenth century, bringing the dishes and foods they were used to.

*"Miss Wall with a basket of greens" on the Windfall*
*near Cranberry Lake, about 1910. P 073488*

*After the Civil War, the economy boomed in the northeastern United States. As cities and industry grew, more and more people sought to escape urban "dust, dirt, and dangers." Many of these "city men" (and their families) found their retreat in the Adirondacks where they could breathe balsam-scented air, drink cold, fresh spring water, and take their own meat from the woods. Like the immigrants who came to settle here, these transients brought with them their own notions of food and its preparation. In the bark lean-tos, grand hotels, and great camps of the late nineteenth century, visitors ate local venison accompanied by French wine.*

*The tourist boom brought with it seasonal jobs, but when the city folk returned home, life—and eating—went on as before for the residents. One of the earliest of the white settlers in the region, John Thurman, called his home a "howling wilderness." Thurman moved to the townships now bearing his name in 1789, and many subsequent generations shared his impression of the region. But the culinary history of the Adirondacks helps us understand that little cash doesn't mean poverty, nor does poor farmland mean starvation. The region's folklore speaks of the "six-weeks' want," that period between the end of winter stores and the first crops of spring. Our research suggests that with gumption, knowledge of the woods, and luck, Adirondackers developed a regional cuisine that took full advantage of both cultivated and wild foods all year long.*

*Today, the food scene is rapidly changing. Approximately 130,000 people live in the Adirondacks all year long. Millions more visit the region every year. Since the second world war, great improvements in roads and communications have enabled Adirondackers to participate in national enthusiasms for exotic ingredients and world cuisines. People living in Long Lake now make sushi with seaweed from Japan and biscotti dipped in chocolate from France. Adirondackers are also buying local, supporting farmers who are rediscovering traditional crops and animals and raising things like goats and fennel that were previously little known in the region. We hope that this book will inspire them, and anyone interested in what makes food special to a place. Enjoy the cultural terroir of Adirondack food.*

# A Note on Historical Sources

The historical notes that accompany some of the recipes tell the story of the Adirondacks. In this day of internet resources, it is all too easy to assume what is "traditional" in one place must be "traditional" everywhere. That sort of assumption can lead to a homogenization of history and a loss of its richness. The Adirondack region shared in the history of New York and the northeast, but its history is also unique. I have come to my conclusions about Adirondack food by studying Adirondack sources, most of them held by the Adirondack Museum in Blue Mountain Lake. Some of these sources, like memoirs and secondary histories, have been published, but others are still in manuscript form. Sifting through diaries and hotel menus is time-consuming, but it has yielded nuggets of information that are unavailable anywhere else. I am particularly grateful to Lucelia Mills Clark, who homesteaded near Cranberry Lake in 1881 and raised eight children with her husband Henry. Every day from 1891 until her death in 1944, Mrs. Clark wrote in her diaries about what she and her family had accomplished. The records of their sugar production, the pounds of butter she churned, what she made of the hogs they slaughtered, and the venison Henry brought home were invaluable in answering the all-important question for the social historian: What did they eat?

All images are courtesy of the Adirondack Museum. Each is identified by its catalog number.

Hallie Bond

# Appetizers

If you'd asked someone in the Adirondacks a century ago what she would like for an appetizer, she wouldn't have known what you were talking about. If she were eating in the dining room of a grand hotel she would expect to start the meal with soup, followed by fish; if she were eating with her family or serving a team of lumberjacks, they would have dived right into the main course. Appetizers are a modern concept, useful to hostesses waiting for the rest of the guests to arrive and wanting those present not to get drunk on cocktails, and to restaurant managers wanting to keep their clients busy while waiting for the main course. This is perhaps the most modern of the chapters in this cookbook, containing Adirondack foods suitable for serving in small bites as twenty-first century appetizers.

*Appetizers are often simplified in camp. The Beale family had crackers and cheese at social hour at the Putnam Camp in Keene Valley in 1952. P 73210*

# Curried Wild Turkey on a Stick

*4 servings*

 While this recipe is intended for wild turkey, domestic turkey could certainly be used.

**16 to 20 (8-inch) bamboo skewers**
**1 pound skinless wild turkey breast**
**2 tablespoons Patak's Mild Curry Paste,**
 **or curry paste of choice**
**2 tablespoons olive oil**

Soak the skewers in warm water for at least an hour to keep them from burning during the cooking process.

Cut the turkey breast into strips, approximately 3 to 4 inches long and $1/2$ inch thick. Place the turkey into a large bowl and add the curry paste and oil; mix thoroughly to evenly coat the meat. Thread 1 piece of marinated turkey onto each skewer.

To cook: you can grill them or sear the skewers in a hot cast iron skillet and finish them in an oven at 350 degrees until the meat turns white, about 5 minutes. These tasty skewers are great on their own, but a simple sauce like minted yogurt makes a great accompaniment.

*These large, ungainly-looking birds were extirpated in the Adirondacks in the 1840s partly because of overhunting and habitat loss, and partly because of the harsh environment. Turkeys depend on food like beechnuts that they scratch up from the forest floor. Heavy snow cover makes foraging difficult. Turkeys have been moving back into the mountains since 1948, however, and as the climate becomes milder they become more abundant.*

# Barbecued Eel

*4 servings*

**1 1/2 pounds fresh eel, cleaned and skinned,
  but still on the bone**
**1 cup Homemade Barbecue Sauce, or barbecue sauce
  of choice**
**1 tablespoon vegetable oil**

Preheat your grill to high heat—I prefer cooking over wood coals or charcoal for the flavor, but a gas grill will also work. Cut the eel into 3-inch pieces and coat with barbecue sauce.

Brush some of the oil onto the grill grates then place pieces of eel on the grill. Cook for 5–6 minutes per side and periodically baste with more sauce. After you have good color on all sides of the eel, remove from the grill and place in a piece of aluminum foil. Add the remaining sauce and fold the foil to make a pouch. Place the pouch back on the grill, close the lid, and allow to cook for another 25–30 minutes or until the eel meat is tender.

## Homemade Barbecue Sauce

*makes 2 1/2 to 3 cups*

**3 tablespoons vegetable oil**
**1 medium onion, minced**
**2 cloves garlic, minced**
**1/4 cup minced green bell pepper**
**1/4 teaspoon red pepper flakes**
**1/2 cup ketchup**
**1/2 cup tomato purée**
**2 ounces cider vinegar**
**2 tablespoons Worcestershire Sauce**
**1/2 cup strong coffee**
**2 tablespoons molasses**
**1/4 cup dark brown sugar**
**2 tablespoons Dijon mustard**
**1 teaspoon dry mustard**
**1/2 teaspoon black pepper**
**1 cup water**
**Kosher salt, to taste**

Heat the oil in a heavy-bottom saucepan over medium heat. Add onion, garlic, bell pepper, and red pepper flakes. Cook until soft but not brown.

Stir in the ketchup, tomato purée, vinegar, Worcestershire sauce, coffee, molasses, brown sugar, Dijon mustard, dry mustard, pepper and water. Bring to a boil then reduce to a simmer. Cook, uncovered, stirring often until it reduces and thickens, about 15 minutes.

Remove from heat; adjust seasoning with salt and additional pepper, if needed. You can serve the sauce as is or cool it down and run through a blender or food processor to make it smooth.

*Modern anglers might never see an eel in the Adirondacks because damming of streams for lumbering and hydropower has restricted the creatures' migration. Eels were once common in the region and anglers since the earliest inhabitants have harvested them for food. You can still see ancient weirs in the shallow streams tumbling out of the Adirondacks. The weirs are formed of long, V-shaped heaps of stones with a gap at the bottom through which the eels swam on their way from their spawning grounds in the Atlantic to the freshwater lakes where they would live out most of their lives. The eel fisher stood at the gap and speared the animals or they were trapped in a basket anchored there.*

*The Iroquois smoked or dried eels, or roasted them. "They cut a stick about three feet long, and as thick as one's thumb," wrote John Bartram in 1743. "They split it about a foot down, and when the eel is gutted, they coil it between the two sides of the stick, and bind the top close which keeps the eel flat, and then stick one end in the ground before a good fire."*

# Smoked Trout with Horseradish Cream

*4 servings*

 You can use store-bought smoked trout or make your own, if you wish.

**12 ounces smoked trout**
**½ cup sour cream**
**1 tablespoon prepared horseradish**
**½ teaspoon freshly grated lemon zest**
**1 teaspoon freshly squeezed lemon juice**
**1 teaspoon chopped fresh dill**
**Salt and pepper, to taste**

Divide the trout into 4 equal portions and arrange on serving plates.

*When he gets all of his thin strips of meat laid on the framework he has made, this man will light the kindling underneath and tend his fire until the smoke and heat has dried the meat to jerky. P 19926*

In a small bowl, add the sour cream, horseradish, lemon zest and juice, dill, and a pinch each of salt and pepper. Mix the ingredients together using a small rubber spatula.

Place some of the horseradish cream on each plate with the smoked trout and serve with your favorite crackers, if desired.

*Cranberry Lake farm wife Lucelia Clark noted in her diary, on October 4, 1913, "men hunted and jerked venison. They have got 12 deer in all." Adirondackers, from the earliest Indians until the days of electric freezers, were faced with the problem of preserving meat. The oldest, and perhaps simplest, method was to cut the meat into thin strips and dry it. In this cool, moist climate, drying was usually done over a wood fire; the smoke itself helped in the preservation process. Today, we don't need to smoke meat for preservation, but we still value the traditional flavor.*

# Pike Fish Cakes

*4 servings*

**I pound skinless pike fillet**
**2 cups water**
**I cup white wine**
**I lemon, juiced**
**2 teaspoons Old Bay Seasoning**
**I egg, lightly whisked**
**¾ cup bread crumbs**
**¼ cup diced onion**
**¼ cup diced green bell pepper**
**Salt and pepper, to taste**
**2 tablespoons olive oil**

*Edwin Noyes, around 1930, in front of Plumley's Camp on Long Lake with a pike he caught. Mr. Noyes stayed at Plumley's, a sort of sportsman's boarding house, while he was working on surveying the Northville-Placid hiking trail. P 33483*

Rinse the pike fillet and set aside. In a small stockpot, add the water, wine, lemon juice, and Old Bay Seasoning. Bring to a boil then reduce to a simmer. Allow to simmer for about 10 minutes to let the flavors develop.

Add the fillet and simmer until done. The flesh will turn white and will be easy to flake apart when done. Carefully remove the fish and allow to drain and cool. When cool, carefully pick out all the bones, break the fish into small pieces, and place in a large bowl.

Add the egg, bread crumbs, onion, bell pepper, and a pinch each of salt and pepper. Gently combine all the ingredients with your hands or a rubber spatula. Divide the mixture into 4 equal portions and form into cakes by first compressing the mix into a ball then carefully flattening.

Preheat a sauté pan over moderate heat, add the oil, and then add the cakes. Cook for approximately 2–3 minutes on each side. Serve while still hot.

*The Adirondack sportsman's fish has always been brook trout. "Brookies" are also known as speckled trout, and are often found in little mountain brooks which are beautiful and fun to explore. They provide exciting fishing for an angler with a fly rod. Other Adirondack fish make excellent eating, too, and when eating is the main aim of fishing, the prehistoric-looking northern pike makes a rewarding meal.*

# Squirrel Cannelloni with Porcini Cream

*4 servings*

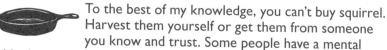 To the best of my knowledge, you can't buy squirrel. Harvest them yourself or get them from someone you know and trust. Some people have a mental block against eating a squirrel, but the ones that come from the forests and farmlands are quite a delicacy. Folks who eat them regularly often refer to them as tree lobsters.

**2 whole cleaned squirrels**
**Salt and pepper, to taste**
**3 tablespoons olive oil**
**6 cloves garlic, peeled**
**I medium Spanish onion, small diced**
**I carrot, peeled and small diced**
**2 ounces dried porcini mushrooms**
**4 sprigs fresh thyme**
**2 sprigs fresh rosemary**
**I cup red wine**
**2 cups reduced veal stock**
**½ cup heavy cream**
**12 pieces cooked pasta sheets, cut into 3½-inch squares**

Season the squirrel with salt and pepper; lightly coat with oil. Sear in a hot cast iron skillet, getting a nice brown color on all sides.

Add the garlic, onion, carrot, mushrooms, thyme, and rosemary. Cook over moderately high heat to get some color on the vegetables then add the wine and use to deglaze the pan. Add the veal stock, bring to a boil, and then reduce to a simmer. Cook over low heat until the meat is tender, about 45 minutes.

Add the cream and stir to incorporate. Adjust seasoning with salt and pepper, if necessary, and remove from the heat and allow to cool until it can be easily handled.

Remove the squirrels from the skillet and carefully pick all the meat from the bones; discard the bones. Strain the braising liquid into a baking dish. Remove the thyme and rosemary stems from the remaining vegetables. Add the vegetables to the reserved meat.

Mix the meat and vegetables together, adding a little braising liquid, if needed. Then place some of the mixture onto each of the pieces of cooked pasta and roll them up. Place the filled rolled pasta, cannelloni, into the baking dish with the liquid and bake until hot and golden brown. Serve immediately.

*With the wild woods just outside their doors, nineteenth-century Adirondackers probably ate more fresh meat than most of their contemporaries. Venison gave the most buck for the bang, but small game appeared regularly on tables, too. Henry Conklin, writing about his boyhood in the southern Adirondacks in the 1840s, remembered an old woman from his neighborhood, one Aunt Peggy Tomkins, who had "two great big dogs and she would take them and go up in the lots on the side hill and dig out woodchucks. The dogs would hole one and then the fun would begin. The dogs both digging and she with hoe or shovel. I tell you, the dirt would fly. When she got after a woodchuck everyone in the neighborhood knew it by the noise she made yelling 'sic 'em Tige, sic 'em Tige'." Aunt Peggy ate the woodchucks, and we can imagine that she enjoyed the sport as well as the food.*

*Young Don Conroy of Wanakena looks like he was ready to do a little small game hunting about 1911. P 14916*

# Grilled Marinated Squab or Pigeon

*4 servings*

**2 whole cleaned squabs or pigeons**
**3 cloves garlic, minced**
**¹/₂ teaspoon chopped fresh thyme**
**¹/₂ teaspoon chopped fresh rosemary**
**I teaspoon chopped fresh flat-leaf parsley**
**2 tablespoons olive oil**
**Salt and pepper, to taste**

Preheat your grill to medium heat. Put the birds in a large bowl. Add the garlic, thyme, rosemary, parsley, oil, salt, and pepper. Toss the birds in the mixture to evenly coat.

Place on the grill, breast side down. Grill for about 5 minutes then turn them on their side. After another 5 minutes, turn them onto their other side. After another 5 minutes, turn them onto their backs. Close the lid and cook for another 5 minutes or until done.

Remove the birds from the grill, place on a platter, and allow to rest at room temperature for 5 minutes. Use a boning knife to cut along the keel bone on both sides and down through the joint where the wing meets the carcass. Then use the knife to follow along the rib cage and down through the hip joint where the leg meets the carcass. You will now have two semi-boneless portions from each bird. Place each portion on a plate and serve.

*Samuel H. Hammond, an Albany lawyer camping out in the Adirondacks for his health in the 1850s, was awakened one morning near Tupper Lake by "a distant roaring; not like a waterfall, or far off thunder, but partaking of both." The noise was made by a vast flock of passenger pigeons whose roosting area covered several acres nearby. Hammond and his guide "breakfasted upon young pigeons, broiled upon the coals. They were very fat and tender, and constituted a pleasant change from fish and venison, which, if the truth must be told, were becoming somewhat stale to us." Hammond took only a few of the birds, but millions more were shot by Adirondackers and others in the northeast in subsequent decades. By the early years of the twentieth century, passenger pigeons were extinct. Gladys Clark may have eaten some of the last Adirondack pigeons, and poor specimens they were. On December 12, 1914, she wrote at Cranberry Lake, "picked the mosquitoes (pigeons) and got them ready to cook." R. C. Pruyn didn't trust to the wild supply. He kept French pigeons for the table at his great camp Santanoni in 1915.*

# Deep-Fried Snapping Turtle

*4 servings*

 Turtles are tough critters, and therefore their meat can be tough, too. Choose a turtle of no more than 10 pounds to help with this issue. Soaking in buttermilk adds flavor, but it is key to helping the tenderization process.

**I cup buttermilk**
**12 ounces boneless turtle meat, cut into 1/2-inch cubes**
**1/2 teaspoon kosher salt**
**2 cups vegetable oil or shortening**
**1/2 cup all-purpose flour**
**1/2 cup cornmeal**
**1/8 teaspoon ground cayenne pepper**
**I teaspoon paprika**
**Salt and pepper, to taste**

In a medium non-metallic bowl, pour the buttermilk over the turtle meat. Add the kosher salt, mix together, cover with plastic wrap, and refrigerate overnight.

Heat the oil in a large frying pan to 360 degrees and preheat the oven to 350 degrees. Strain the turtle meat and discard the buttermilk.

In a small bowl, combine the flour, cornmeal, cayenne pepper, paprika, and a pinch each of salt and pepper. Mix gently to combine all the ingredients.

Dredge the meat in the flour mixture. Shake off the excess flour and carefully place the turtle pieces in the hot oil. Fry until golden brown then turn the pieces to brown the other side. When all sides are browned, remove the pieces from the oil, place them on a baking sheet, and bake for 10 minutes. Season with additional salt and pepper, if desired, and serve. Any number of dipping sauces will work well with fried turtle; I like aioli or hot sauce with mine.

On September 30, 1894, dinner at Paul Smith's Hotel started with Green Turtle Soup à l'Anglaise; in the same era, the Prospect House on Blue Mountain Lake and the Riverside Inn in Saranac Lake served Consommé of Green Turtle, accompanied by sherry. These hotels were making a statement about how cosmopolitan they were, as the green turtle, a sea turtle, was standard fare at grand establishments in cities. All three of these Adirondack hotels were reached by railroads in the 1890s and could serve just about anything dished up by their city competition.

The snapping turtle is common in the Adirondacks, and is the state reptile of New York. It can provide a large amount of meat (snappers can weigh up to 35 pounds), but a large one can inflict a significant amount of damage with its sharp, rapidly darting beak.

# Sautéed Ramps with White Wine

*4 servings*

**1 pound fresh whole ramps, cleaned**
**1 tablespoon olive oil**
**¼ cup white wine**
**Salt and pepper, to taste**
**1 tablespoon butter, optional**

Cut the bulbous bottoms off all the ramps and set aside. Cut the green leafy portions into 1-inch pieces.

Heat a sauté pan over high heat. Add the oil then immediately add the bottom portions of the ramps; sauté, stirring periodically to keep them from burning. You should get some color on them, but avoid overdoing it.

Add the wine. Cook until the wine is reduced by half then add the greens of the ramps. Add a pinch each of salt and pepper. Cook until the greens are wilted. Add the butter, if using. Serve as soon as the butter melts.

*This elegant treatment of a wild food would be appropriate for the outdoor dining room at Camp Pine Knot, pictured here in the mid-1880s. P 1602*

Ramps, wild members of the onion family, are some of the first green things to appear in the woods in the springtime. By the time the leaves are coming out on the trees, they turn yellow, fall over, and pretty much disappear until the next season. The bulbs are found 3–6 inches underground, and are best dug with a shovel, rather than pulled. Ramps grow wild and Adirondackers since the Abenaki and Iroquois have eaten them.

# Buttermilk-Fried Rabbit Loin

*4 Servings*

Rabbit is available in some grocery stores, it can be purchased through specialty stores like Adventure In Food Trading Company, or it can be harvested.

**4 boneless rabbit loins**
**¾ cup buttermilk**
**I cup vegetable oil**
**Salt and pepper, to taste**
**¾ cup all-purpose flour**
**¼ teaspoon dried ground sage**
**½ teaspoon garlic powder**
**½ teaspoon onion powder**
**¼ teaspoon kosher salt**
**¼ teaspoon ground black pepper**

Place the rabbit loins in a non-metallic dish and cover with buttermilk. Cover with plastic wrap and refrigerate overnight.

*Godfrey Dewey, developer of the Lake Placid Club, stands at right in this snapshot of a successful rabbit hunt in 1922. P 1166*

Heat the oil in a large skillet to 375 degrees. Remove the rabbit loins from the buttermilk and sprinkle them with salt and pepper.

In a small bowl, combine the flour, sage, garlic powder, onion powder, salt, and pepper. Whisk gently to incorporate all the ingredients. Dredge the rabbit in the flour mixture and shake off any excess.

Carefully place in skillet and fry until golden brown then turn the pieces over and fry the other side. Remove from oil, place on a paper towel to drain, and allow to rest for 2–3 minutes before serving.

*Buttermilk is a product of churning butter—it is the liquid left after the butter "comes," or solidifies in the churn. There was thus a lot of it in butter-making families. Because it is quite acidic, it works well in baked goods leavened with baking soda—the combination of the two creates carbon dioxide which raises the bread. In this recipe, the lactic acid tenderizes the rabbit.*

# Duck Leg Confit

*4 servings*

 Duck is available in some grocery stores and it, along with the rendered fat, can be purchased through specialty stores like Adventure In Food Trading Company out of Albany, New York, or it can be harvested.

**8 cloves garlic, peeled**
**1 shallot, peeled and sliced**
**6 sprigs fresh thyme**
**3 sprigs fresh rosemary**
**2 teaspoons coarsely ground black pepper**
**$^1/_2$ cup kosher salt**
**$^1/_2$ cup brown sugar**
**4 whole duck legs, with thighs and skin intact**
**1 quart rendered duck fat**

Place the garlic, shallot, thyme, rosemary, pepper, salt, and brown sugar in a food processor. Start the processor by pulsing at first then allow to run for about a minute to incorporate all the ingredients.

Place about a third of this mixture in the bottom of a glass baking dish. Place the duck legs on top then completely cover the legs with the remainder of the mixture. Cover with plastic wrap and refrigerate.

After 24 hours, remove the duck legs from the mixture. Rinse them briefly under cold water to remove any of the remaining curing mixture. Pat dry and set aside.

Preheat oven to 275 degrees.

Melt the duck fat in an 8- x 8- x 4-inch dish in the oven. Once the duck fat is liquefied, carefully submerge the duck legs in the fat. Return the dish to the oven and cook until the duck is very tender, approximately $2^1/_2$ hours. When finished, the duck can be refrigerated in its own fat for up to a couple of weeks.

When you are ready to serve the confit, remove the duck legs from the excess fat. Heat a tablespoon or two of the rendered fat in a cast iron skillet over moderate heat. Place the duck legs in the hot fat, skin side down. Cook until nicely browned then flip over and brown the other side. When the legs are evenly browned and warmed through, they are ready to serve. The left over duck fat can be strained, refrigerated, and reused at a later date.

*For Sunday dinner in the depths of the Depression, on October 25, 1931, a family in Thurman sat down to a big spread of sixteen dishes, only one of which was meat—pressed meat. Pressed meat is a close though plebeian relation of the confit of this recipe. Both confit and pressed meat originated as ways to preserve meat by cooking it and isolating it from the air.*

*Confit, meat cooked and preserved in its own fat, is a French invention, worthy of the cosmopolitan tables of Adirondack grand hotels and great camps. The pressed meat of the Thurman dinner was probably made up of bits and shreds leftover from butchering, prepared with spices, perhaps, and cooked with broth to the jelly stage. The mixture was put into a loaf pan and weighed down while cooling.*

# Roasted Pear with Melted Brie, Spiced Walnuts, and Frisée

*4 servings*

## Pears

**2 fresh Bartlett pears**
**1 sprig fresh thyme**
**2 teaspoons olive oil**
**Kosher salt and freshly ground black pepper, to taste**

## Spiced Walnuts

**3 ounces walnut pieces**
**1 teaspoon olive oil**
**1 teaspoon sugar**
**Dash ground cayenne pepper**
**Dash ground allspice**

## Frisée

**1 tablespoon olive oil**
**1 teaspoon white balsamic vinegar**
**Salt and pepper, to taste**
**1 head Frisée lettuce, washed and shaken dry**

**6 ounces Brie cheese**

**Pears:** Preheat oven to 350 degrees. Wash and peel the pears then carefully remove the core and seeds with a melon baller. Cut off the stems and slice the pears in half lengthwise.

Strip the thyme from the stem and chop the leaves. Coat the pears with the oil then sprinkle with the thyme, salt, and pepper.

Place the pears, flat side down on a baking sheet and roast until tender, about 20 minutes. Remove from the oven and allow to cool to room temperature for serving.

**Spiced Walnuts:** Preheat oven to 350 degrees. In a small bowl, toss the walnut pieces in the oil. Add the sugar, cayenne, and allspice. Toss again until evenly coated. Spread the coated nuts on a baking sheet in a single layer and toast until the sugar melts and coats the nuts, about 5–7 minutes. Remove from the oven, stir gently with a spatula to free them from sticking to the pan, and allow to cool at room temperature.

**Frisée:** Place the oil, vinegar, and a pinch each of salt and pepper in a medium bowl then whisk together. Add the frisée and toss lightly to coat. Keep chilled until ready to serve.

Preheat the broiler. Slice the Brie into $1/4$-inch-thick pieces and arrange about $1^1/2$ ounces of cheese in a single layer near the center of 4 oven-safe plates. Melt the cheese until the cheese just starts to melt and run. Remove from the heat, place a half pear on top, sprinkle with walnuts, and garnish with the salad.

*If you want to give this dish a locavore touch, go out and pick some hazelnuts, as Julia Baker Kellogg did near Minerva in 1865. She got 2 quarts on that expedition with her sister. You could also use beechnuts which are common in the Adirondacks and were gathered by the Iroquois and Algonquin who put them in breads, soups, or sagamité, a sort of cornmeal mush.*

# Tempura-Fried Fiddlehead Ferns

*4 servings*

 Fiddleheads are one of first produce items available each and every spring in the Northeast. They grow wild and usher in the spring by offering foragers and diners a taste of the new season. There are many different fern varietals that grow in New York, but only the ostrich fern is suitable for the table and carries the name fiddlehead. If you're not sure what to pick, go with someone who does; or find a reliable source to buy them from.

**1 egg**
**¹/₂ teaspoon kosher salt**
**¹/₂ teaspoon ground black pepper**
**1 cup club soda**
**¹/₂ cup Sprite or Sierra Mist**
**3 cups all-purpose flour, divided**
**12 ounces fiddlehead ferns, washed and blanched**
**Vegetable oil, enough for at least 2 inches of oil in your pan**
**Salt, to taste**

Place the egg, salt, and pepper in a large bowl and lightly whisk. Add the club soda and Sprite and lightly whisk to incorporate ingredients. Add about 1 cup of the flour and whisk gently. You are looking for light batter consistency and do not want to overwork the flour. Add a little more flour, if necessary.

Preheat oil to 350 degrees in a deep frying pan.

Dip the ferns, one at a time, in the tempura batter and then drop them in the remaining flour. Shake off any excess flour, place in hot oil, and fry until golden brown. Remove from the oil, allow to drain, sprinkle with salt, and serve while hot with Spicy Chile Aioli dipping sauce.

# Spicy Chile Aioli

*makes about 1 cup*

**1 lemon, juiced**
**2 cloves garlic, peeled**
**2 teaspoons white vinegar**
**1 cup mayonnaise**
**$\frac{1}{2}$ teaspoon kosher salt**
**$\frac{1}{2}$ teaspoon ground white pepper**
**2 teaspoons sambal oelek (Thai chile paste)**

Place the lemon juice, garlic, and vinegar in a food processor and run on high speed to make a smooth mixture. Add the mayonnaise, salt, and pepper. Run on high speed again to make a make a smooth sauce. Fold in the sambal oelek, chill, and serve as a dipping sauce.

*"Chillie Sauce" appears on Adirondack hotel menus in the 1880s and 1890s, but it doesn't much resemble the exotic ethnic chile sauces modern Americans are used to. In the 1930s, Anna Scripter of Thurman made hers with tomatoes, onions, green bell peppers, vinegar, cinnamon, cloves, mustard, and some unidentified "red pepper."*

*Aioli and tempura, as well as chiles, have been popularized in this country in the revival of interest in ethnic foods in the last fifty years or so. The concept of battering and frying is a classic Adirondack method, though. Fiddleheads are also a traditional regional treat.*

# Soups

The hearty soups in this section keep alive an ancient Adirondack tradition of one-pot meals. Even before the Indians had iron and brass kettles through trade with Europeans, they cooked food in liquid by placing rocks heated in the fire into birchbark containers or hollowed out wooden vessels. Strange as it may seem, one eighteenth-century observer reported seeing birchbark containers full of food being suspended over the fire—he said that as long as the edge of the bark wasn't exposed to the flame it couldn't burn. The thick Indian soup, available on the fire all day, was *sagamité*—water and cornmeal with whatever fish, meat, squash, beans, or greens were available.

A pot of food cooked in liquid was popular with homesteaders, too, and has always been an ideal dish for busy working people.

*Guides Wallace Emerson and Reuben Cary prepare a meal of some sort of soup or stew in Brandreth Park about 1900. P 900*

The chefs at great camps and hotels in the nineteenth century made more refined soups for the first course of the multi-course meals of the Victorian era. Consommé (a clear soup) was standard, and green (sea) turtle soup showed off the chef's access to far-away sources of ingredients.

# Mohawk Soup

*8 servings*

**2 tablespoons olive oil**
**12 ounces smoked boneless pork chops, diced**
**¾ cup diced yellow onion**
**¾ cup shredded cabbage**
**¾ cup peeled and diced rutabaga**
**¾ cup peeled and diced butternut squash**
**1 quart chicken stock**
**1 (19-ounce) can red kidney beans, drained and rinsed**
**1 (19-ounce) can hominy**
**1 cup fresh spinach,**
**chopped**
**Salt and pepper, to taste**

Heat the oil in a large stock pot over medium heat. Add the pork and onion. Cook until the onion is soft. Add the cabbage, rutabaga, squash, stock, kidney beans, and hominy. Bring to a boil then reduce to a simmer. Cook until the rutabaga is tender, about 25 minutes.

Stir in the spinach and allow it to wilt. Adjust seasoning with salt and pepper and serve.

*This circa 1920 view from the top of the Blue Mountain Hill in Hamilton County, near the site of the present day Adirondack Museum, gives an idea of the vistas common in the region when more people were farmers. P 14563*

A key ingredient in this soup is corn that has been treated with lye, a process called nixtamalization. This removes the hull and keeps the corn from germinating, and also makes the corn more nutritious and easier to grind. Modern cooks know this product as hominy. To treat corn, Indians and white men alike made lye by leaching hardwood ashes with water, and then boiled the corn in this very alkaline solution. When the hulls started to slip off the kernels, the corn was drained and then washed and the hulls rubbed off—ideally in running water. The Mohawk used splint baskets partially submerged in a stream for the washing.

# Vegetable Soup in its Own Broth

*4 servings*

1 tablespoon olive oil
4 cloves garlic, thinly sliced
¼ cup diced red onion
1 bay leaf
½ teaspoon fresh thyme
½ cup diced yellow summer squash
½ cup diced zucchini
½ cup diced red bell pepper
½ cup frozen corn
½ cup diced Roma tomato
½ cup white wine
2 cups tomato juice
1 cup water
Salt and pepper, to taste

Heat the oil over medium heat in a large saucepan. Add the garlic, stir with a wooden spoon, and cook until it starts to turn golden brown. Add the onion and bay leaf; cook until the onion is soft.

Add the thyme, squash, zucchini, bell pepper, corn, and tomato. Stir to combine and cook for another 3–4 minutes. Add the wine and cook for about 5 minutes then add the tomato juice and water.

Bring to a boil then reduce to simmer and cook until all the vegetables are tender. Adjust seasoning with salt and pepper to your liking and serve.

*The Mohawk, living in their palisaded "castles" along the Mohawk River, are the best known Indians in Adirondack history. The Western Abenaki used the region, as well. The Abenaki tended to move around more than the Mohawk, but they, too, grew beans, squash, and corn, which they referred to as "the woman with the golden hair." Both the Mohawk and the Abenaki made soups like this without a meat broth when they didn't have meat or fish.*

# Potato and Leek Soup

*8 servings*

**2 tablespoons butter**
**3 cloves garlic, crushed**
**1½ cups washed and sliced**
  **leeks (white part only)**
**2 bay leaves**
**2½ cups chef or russet**
  **potatoes, washed,**
  **peeled, and diced**
**2 teaspoons kosher salt**
**1 teaspoon ground white**
  **pepper**
**1 quart chicken broth**
**1 cup heavy cream**

*Henry and Lucelia Clark's grandchildren—and a pet. P73432*

Melt the butter over medium heat in a large stock pot. Add the garlic, leeks, and bay leaves. Cook over low to medium heat, stirring often until the leeks are soft but have no added color.

Add the potatoes, salt, white pepper, broth, and cream. Bring to a boil then reduce to a simmer. Cook until the potatoes are very soft, about 45 minutes.

Remove from the heat and remove the bay leaves. Purée in small batches in a blender until smooth. Place each batch into another pot until it is all done. Return the pot to the heat and bring to boil while stirring constantly to prevent scorching. Serve immediately.

*Potatoes do well in the Adirondacks, and families traditionally depended on them. Like bread, potatoes appeared on the table nearly every day, no doubt prepared in as many ways as the cook could invent. Julia Baker Kellogg, in Minerva, and Lucelia Clark, near Cranberry Lake, put in their cellars between 60 and 80 bushels of potatoes a year a century ago. Caring for the crop was a family affair. On June 10, 1906, Mrs. Clark recorded that her "grandkids picked potato bugs. H[enry, her husband] told them he would give them 5 cts p 100 & they got about 800 apiece."*

# Ham and Bean Soup

*8 servings*

2 tablespoons vegetable oil
6 cloves garlic, sliced
1 cup diced yellow onion
2 bay leaves
1 teaspoon fresh thyme
1 teaspoon fresh rosemary
2 smoked ham hocks
2 quarts chicken broth
1 pound mixed dried beans, soaked overnight in water
1/2 cup peeled and diced carrots
1/2 cup diced celery
2 tablespoons chopped flat-leaf parsley
Salt and pepper, to taste

Heat the oil in a large stock pot over medium heat. Add the garlic, onion, and bay leaves. Cook until the onion is soft but not browned.

Add the thyme, rosemary, ham hocks, and chicken broth. Simmer until the meat on the hocks starts to get tender, about an hour.

Drain the soaked beans and add them to the pot along with the carrots and celery. Simmer until the beans are tender, about 30–40 minutes.

Remove the hocks, pick the meat from the bones, and return the meat to the soup. Add the parsley and adjust seasoning with salt and pepper before serving.

*These pigs fed people in the paper mill
town of Piercefield in 1910. P 9237*

*Most ham and ham hocks you buy today are but pale shadows
of the pork preserved by Adirondackers a century ago. Today,
processors salt and smoke pork lightly (or even add artificial
smoke flavoring) more to add flavor than to preserve the meat.
Traditionally, salt and smoke were essential for turning a fresh,
thick pork haunch into a preserved ham. First, you rubbed a
mixture of sugar, saltpeter, and salt thoroughly into the ham then
set it to cure, or partially dry, in a crock in a cool place for a month
or more. When the ham was cured, you smoked it for several days,
drying it further. Later on, when you went to cook a ham like this,
you had to soak it for a day in several changes of water and then
scrub it all over to remove salt and surface mold.*

# Creamy Corn Chowder

*8 servings*

 To get more corn flavor use fresh corn on the cob. Remove the kernels from the cob and reserve. Steep the cobs in the chicken broth and heavy cream over medium heat for 45 minutes. Strain the liquid and use in the recipe. This will give you the maximum amount of corn flavor for your soup.

**½ pound bacon, cut into small pieces**
**¾ cup diced yellow onion**
**4 cloves garlic, chopped**
**3 cups frozen corn**
**I cup peeled and diced potatoes**
**¾ cup diced celery**
**½ cup diced red bell pepper**
**½ cup diced green bell pepper**
**6 tablespoons all-purpose flour**
**3 tablespoons chopped fresh thyme**
**I teaspoon cayenne pepper**
**I tablespoon sugar**
**I quart chicken broth**
**I quart heavy cream**
**Salt and pepper, to taste**

Render the bacon over medium heat in a large stock pot. When the bacon has released most of its fat and the meat just starts to brown, add the onion and garlic. Cook over medium heat until the onion and garlic are soft, but do not let them get brown. Stir occasionally with a wooden spoon.

Add the corn, potatoes, celery, and bell peppers. Stir to combine and cook over medium heat for 3–4 minutes. Add the flour and stir until the flour absorbs the bacon fat and moisture. Add the thyme, cayenne, and sugar. Stir.

Using a whisk, slowly add a small amount of the broth. Whisk gently to prevent lumping of the flour mixture as you add the remaining broth. Whisk in the cream. Bring to boil then reduce to a simmer and cook until the potatoes are tender, about 15 minutes. Adjust seasoning with salt and pepper and serve.

This dish unites corn, an ancient food long used in the Adirondacks, with milk, a food from the traditions of the white settlers. The final result, a corn soup, has roots in both traditions. The earliest French explorers in the region reported that the most common dish in the Indian camps and villages they visited was sagamité which, in its basic form, was just cornmeal cooked in water. The Iroquois often added squash, beans, smoked fish, or meat to this thick mixture. White settlers adopted the dish, added salt, and called it "samp" or mush. Lucelia Clark, who fed a large family near Cranberry Lake, wrote triumphantly in her diary on April 15, 1917, "Had corn meal mush for supper at 8 cts per lb. Cheap!!!"

Mrs. Clark also might have made this chowder for her family for she, like most other Adirondack farmers, kept milk cows. The Clarks churned most of their milk into butter which they ate or sold. Some of the milk found its way into cooking, and some was drunk fresh.

# Pulled Chicken and Root Vegetable Soup

*8 servings*

**2 tablespoons olive oil**
**1 cup diced yellow onion**
**4 cloves garlic, sliced**
**½ cup diced celery**
**½ cup peeled and diced carrots**
**½ cup peeled and diced parsnips**
**½ cup peeled and diced rutabaga**
**½ cup peeled and diced celery root**
**1 roasted whole chicken (about 1½ pounds)**
**1½ quarts chicken broth**
**2 teaspoons chopped fresh thyme**
**2 teaspoons chopped fresh rosemary**
**Salt and pepper, to taste**

Heat the oil in a large stock pot over medium heat. Add the onion and garlic and stir. Cook until the onion is soft. Add the celery, carrots, parsnips, rutabaga, and celery root. Stir and continue to cook over low heat for 5–6 minutes.

While the vegetables are cooking, peel the skin off the chicken and set it aside. Pull the chicken meat off the bones and cut into small pieces. Add the pulled meat to the pot. Save the skin and bones to make your next batch of chicken broth.

Add the broth, thyme, and rosemary. Bring to a boil then reduce to a simmer and cook until all the vegetables are tender. Adjust seasoning with salt and pepper and serve.

*Root cellar of the Persons family in the woods near Blue Mountain Lake about 1904. P 14704*

*Root vegetables like carrots, parsnips, turnips, onions, beets, and potatoes all grow well in the cool climate of the Adirondacks. Root vegetables are good keepers, too. If you have the right conditions—cool temperatures and enough humidity to keep them from drying out but not molding—you can store root vegetables from harvest to springtime. Adirondack homes from great camps to log huts had root cellars for this purpose. In some houses the root cellar was literally a cellar—the space under the house. You might fetch the potatoes by going down a stair, or you might just open a trap door in the kitchen. Many root cellars were underground spaces outside the house.*

*Root cellar at the Garvin family's great camp estate, Kamp Kill Kare 1955. P 9549*

# Howling Bear Chili

*8 servings*

 To procure bear meat, you either have to know a hunter who will share it with you or harvest it yourself. If you can't find bear meat, beef can be substituted.

**2 tablespoons vegetable oil**
**¾ pound boneless bear rump roast, cut into ½-inch cubes**
**I cup diced yellow onion**
**6 cloves garlic, sliced**
**¾ pound ground bear meat**
**I tablespoon ground cumin**
**2 tablespoons chile powder**
**I teaspoon dried red pepper flakes, optional**
**I teaspoon kosher salt**
**I teaspoon ground black pepper**
**I (28-ounce) can crushed tomatoes**
**2 cups tomato juice**
**I cup water**
**I (28-ounce) can white beans**
**½ cup diced green bell pepper**
**Salt and pepper, to taste**

Heat the oil in a large stock pot over high heat, add the cubed bear meat and brown on all sides; add the onion and garlic. Reduce heat to medium and cook until the onions are soft. Add the ground bear meat, cumin, chile powder, red pepper flakes, kosher salt, and ground pepper. Stir with a wooden spoon and use it to break up the ground meat.

Add the crushed tomatoes, tomato juice, water, white beans, and bell pepper. Bring to a boil then reduce to a simmer. Cook over low heat until the cubed bear meat is tender, about 45 minutes to an hour. Adjust seasoning with salt and pepper, if necessary, and serve while piping hot.

Adirondackers hunted bear for sport, for food, and because bears could be pests. In a letter written in 1858, a Ticonderoga farmer reported a hunt that was organized to find a bear rampaging through a neighbor's cornfield. Sixty people and their dogs drove the bear to a swamp where he was cornered and shot. The "old he bair, the one that has been a terror to the farmers on both sides of the mountain" weighed 402 pounds. The meat and proceeds from selling the hide (nine dollars) were divided among all sixty hunters—hardly enough for a stew in any one household, but perhaps a ceremonial triumph over the corn vandal.

Bear is not always thought of as food. It has a reputation for tasting unpleasantly "gamey" and for carrying trichinosis, but properly handled and cooked, it can be a delicious addition to the table. Bears have a lot of fat on them which was not scorned by earlier cooks. The rendered fat is semi-solid and spoonable and makes good biscuits.

Stella Otis with the black bear she shot in 1912. P 11059

# Roasted Tomato and Basil Soup

*8 servings*

**12 Roma tomatoes**
**4 tablespoons olive oil, divided**
**1 teaspoon kosher salt**
**1 teaspoon ground black pepper**
**8 cloves garlic, sliced**
**1 cup white wine**
**3 cups tomato juice**
**1 cup water**
**8 leaves fresh basil, chopped**
**Salt and pepper, to taste**

Preheat oven to 400 degrees. Use the tip of a paring knife to remove the stem end of each tomato. Place the tomatoes on a baking sheet, drizzle with 2 tablespoons oil, then rub the oil on the tomatoes to evenly coat. Sprinkle with kosher salt and ground pepper. Roast until they start to get soft, approximately 15 minutes.

Remove the tomatoes from the oven and allow to cool enough so that you can handle them. Peel the skin from the tomatoes and discard. Roughly chop the tomatoes and set aside.

In a large stock pot, heat the remaining oil over medium heat. Add the garlic and cook until it turns golden brown. Add the reserved tomatoes then the wine; stir. Cook down until the wine is reduced by half. Add the tomato juice and water. Bring to boil then reduce to simmer; cook for 10–15 minutes. Add basil, stir, and then taste. Adjust seasoning with salt and pepper, if necessary, and serve chunky style or purée to serve it smooth.

Any gathering of Adirondack gardeners today will end up discussing the difficulties of growing tomatoes in the mountains. Lucelia Clark, gardening and feeding a large family near Cranberry Lake in the early twentieth century, could have joined in. Some years she pickled the unripe tomatoes she had to rescue from the frost. On September 1, 1906, "for an experiment," she hit on a way of keeping her plants safe with a kerosene lamp from the house. "Hard frost last night," she wrote in her diary, "but we had the tent over the tomatoes & cukes & kept a light burning all night and they did not freeze."

This Old Forge man protected his seedlings from early cold weather by cold frames. P 70571

# Maple and Spiced Creamy Butternut Soup

*8 servings*

**2 tablespoons olive oil**
**I cup diced yellow onion**
**4 cloves garlic, crushed**
**3 cups roasted butternut squash pulp***
**1/2 teaspoon dried ground ginger**
**1/4 teaspoon ground clove**
**1/4 teaspoon ground allspice**
**3/4 cup pure maple syrup**
**I quart chicken broth**
**I cup heavy cream**
**Salt and pepper, to taste**

Heat the oil in a large stock pot over medium heat. Add the onion and garlic and cook over medium heat until soft, but with no color. Stir occasionally with a wooden spoon.

Add the squash, ginger, clove, allspice, and maple syrup. Stir then add the stock and cream. Bring to a boil then reduce to a simmer. Cook until everything is soft, about 30 minutes.

Remove from heat and carefully purée in a blender in small batches. Do not fill more than 2/3 full to prevent the hot liquid from coming out of the blender. Pulse the mixture at first then run on high speed to make it smooth. Place each batch into another pot until all the batches are done.

Return the soup to the heat and stir to incorporate to achieve an even consistency. Adjust seasoning with salt and pepper, if necessary, and serve while hot.

* To roast a butternut squash, start by cutting the squash in half lengthwise. Scoop out the seeds with a spoon. Rub the squash inside and out with olive oil, salt, and pepper. Place the squash cut side down on a baking sheet and bake in a 350 degree oven until soft. Remove from the oven and allow to cool enough that you can handle. Use a spoon to scrape the pulp away from the skin.

One of A.A. Low's three state-of-the-art sugar houses. Note the sap pipes going directly into the second story. P20993

The Québec sugar makers of Canada are the OPEC of world maple syrup these days, and in this country, the center of production is Vermont. The Adirondacks also have a long and honorable history in the business. For many farm families, maple sugar was like so many other farm products—produced primarily for the family with any surplus sold for income. Farmers Henry and Lucelia Clark, with eight children to feed (and to help with the sugaring work), hung 810 buckets in 1909, which gave them 187 gallons of syrup and 350 pounds of cake sugar. They sold what they didn't use in neighboring Cranberry Lake. At the same time, A.A. Low, New York entrepreneur and heir to a great China Trade fortune, established a state-of-the-art sugaring business on his land north of Long Lake. He had three sugarbushes, each with its own steam-heated, marble-floored sugar house, and he packaged his products in custom-made bottles. Low's workmen, John Rivet and James Hill, invented the continuous-flow evaporator most sugarmakers use today, and Low pioneered the marketing of maple sugar as candy.

# Yellow Perch Fillets in Broth— "Poor Man's Shrimp"

*4 servings*

 Yellow perch are a delicious pan fish found in many fresh water lakes and rivers throughout the Adirondacks. If you choose not to catch your own, or have someone catch them for you, you can substitute using perch fillets from the grocery store, although store-bought fillets will be from ocean perch. To make your own fish broth, save the bones from the fish after you have filleted them. Place the bones in a saucepan and cover them with water, add some carrots, celery, and onion and simmer for 1 hour.

**2 tablespoons olive oil**
**1/2 cup chopped yellow onion**
**4 cloves garlic, sliced**
**1/2 cup diced celery**
**1 tablespoon Old Bay Seasoning**
**1/2 teaspoon celery seed**
**1 teaspoon fresh thyme, chopped**
**1 cup white wine**
**1 lemon**
**3 cups fish broth**
**1/2 pound boneless, skinless yellow perch fillets**
**Salt and pepper, to taste**

Heat the olive oil in a large stock pot over medium heat. Add the onion and garlic. Cook until the onion is soft, about 5 minutes. Add the celery, seasoning, celery seed, thyme, and wine. Stir, bring to a boil, and reduce the wine by half. Reduce heat to a simmer.

Roll the lemon on a cutting board with the palm of your hand, pressing firmly but not hard enough to break the lemon open. Cut the lemon in half, squeeze the juice into the pot, and then drop the two halves in as well. Add the fish broth and simmer for 10 minutes. Remove the lemon halves and any seeds.

Add the fillets and cook over medium heat until just done. The fillets are done when they turn opaque white and start to flake apart. Adjust seasoning with salt and pepper and serve.

Yellow perch are often the first fish caught by young anglers. They are common in Adirondack lakes, caught easily by children on their summer camp docks or cruising around in a flat-bottomed rowboat. Most city sportsmen of the nineteenth century scorned any fish but trout, but perch and other pan fish, like sunfish and little bass, can be a delicious treat.

James Fynmore, "Young Fishermen" at Adirondack Woodcraft Camp, ca. 1960. P 15938

# Salads

For much of the late twentieth century, "salad" meant fresh leaves (usually lettuce) with dressing served at the beginning of the meal. The recipes in this section take us back to a more traditional meaning of "salad," which is to say vegetables or even meat cooked and served cold with dressing. Diners at places like Bisby Lodge, a century ago, ate dressed lettuces, cucumbers, cabbages and other vegetables, and sometimes these dishes appeared at the beginning of the meal with relishes like chow-chow and sometimes they brought up the tail end of the meal, just before the pastry course. Ordinary Adirondackers gathered their green salad makings from the woods when they could. Daisy Dalaba Allen, who grew up on a farm in Baker's Mills during the Depression, remembered gathering pig weed, red root, red dock, dandelions, cowslips, and "the little onion-type part of the cattail."

*Garden at Bisby Lodge, Bisby Lake, 1910.*
*89.57.28*

# Dandelion Salad

*4 servings*

 The first dandelion greens of the year will be the most tender and sweet. As the season goes on, the greens get tougher and more bitter.

**12 ounces dandelion greens**
**1 small red onion, thinly sliced**
**12 cherry tomatoes, cut**
**in half**
**1 teaspoon finely**
**chopped shallot**
**1 teaspoon Dijon**
**mustard**
**1 tablespoon red wine**
**vinegar**
**3 tablespoons olive oil**
**Salt and pepper, to taste**

Place the greens, red onion, and tomatoes in a large bowl.

Place the shallot, mustard, vinegar, oil, and a pinch each of salt and pepper in a small jar. Tighten the lid and shake vigorously. Pour the dressing over the greens, toss gently to coat, and serve.

*This unidentified woman gathering greens near Saranac Lake might say, as Lucelia Clark did on May 24, 1913, "dug dandylions—loads of them—wheelbarrow loads!" P28360*

The Iroquois and the Algonquin roaming the Adirondacks before contact didn't know the pleasures of dandelions. Europeans introduced this plant, which many of us regard as a weed, before the seventeenth century. It spread—like a weed—and subsequent settlers in the Adirondacks welcomed these fresh spring greens at the end of a long winter when they were heartily tired of potatoes and sauerkraut as their only vegetables. On April 23, 1914, Lucelia Clark "picked some dandylions for dinner tomorrow" on her place near Cranberry Lake. Mrs. Clark usually cooked her "dandylions."

# Bulgur Wheat with Vegetables

*4 servings*

**2 cups cooked bulgur wheat, chilled**
**¹/₂ cup diced tomato**
**¹/₂ cup diced cucumber**
**¹/₄ cup diced red onion**
**¹/₄ cup diced yellow squash**
**¹/₄ cup diced zucchini**
**¹/₂ cup diced red apple**
**1 tablespoon chopped fresh dill**
**2 teaspoons chopped fresh tarragon**
**3 tablespoons cider vinegar**
**5 tablespoons olive oil**
**1 teaspoon sugar**
**Salt and pepper, to taste**

In a non-metallic bowl, combine the bulgur wheat, tomato, cucumber, onion, squash, zucchini, apple, dill, and tarragon. Toss gently to incorporate.

In a small jar, combine the vinegar, oil, sugar, and a pinch each of salt and pepper. Tighten the lid and shake vigorously. Pour the dressing over the salad, tossing gently to incorporate. Cover with plastic wrap and refrigerate for at least 1 hour before serving.

*In the early twentieth century, Medora Hooper established a small school for her daughters and the children of workers at her husband's remote garnet mine near North River. Medora must have been aware of the growing Progressive Education movement, which valued gardens and learning by doing, and the children planted a vegetable garden in 1913 as part of their school. P50860*

*This is a thoroughly modern version of an ancient Adirondack dish—grain and vegetables. Mohawk women prepared* sagamité, *a mixture of coarse cornmeal and vegetables (sometimes with meat) many times a week.*

# Pickled Vegetables

*8 servings*

2 cups cauliflower florets
2 cups broccoli florets
1 cup radishes, quartered
1 handful green beans, stems removed
1 handful yellow wax beans, stems removed
2 cups peeled and sliced carrots (cut into coin shapes)
1 bunch spring onions (scallions), cut into pieces
6 cloves garlic
3 cups cider vinegar
3 cups water
¾ cup sugar
½ cup kosher salt
2 teaspoons whole black peppercorns
1 tablespoon whole mustard seeds
2 bay leaves
3 whole cloves
1 teaspoon celery seed
1 teaspoon fennel seed

Place the cauliflower, broccoli, radishes, beans, carrots, onions, and garlic in a large glass jar. If you don't have a big enough jar, a mixing bowl will also work.

In a large stock pot, combine the vinegar, water, sugar, salt, peppercorns, mustard seeds, bay leaves, cloves, celery seed, and fennel seed. Bring to a boil and cook for about 5 minutes. Pour the hot liquid over the vegetables and let stand, uncovered, until the mixture cools to room temperature. Cover and refrigerate at least overnight.

*Adirondackers of the nineteenth and twentieth centuries pickled all sorts of foods—meat as well as fruits and vegetables. A spoonful of pickled beets or cucumbers might be the only bright thing on the dinner plate from November to May. Lucelia Clark pickled cucumbers (what most people today think of as "pickles"), beans, green tomatoes, melon rinds, and corn. Because she lived after glass jars became common, Mrs. Clark canned her pickles by treating them with high heat. This cooks the pickles, however, and the result isn't as crunchy as the uncooked pickles in the recipe.*

# Seven Bean Salad

*8 servings*

1 ½ cups fresh green beans, snipped
   and cut into 1-inch pieces
1 ½ cups fresh yellow wax beans, snipped
   and cut into 1-inch pieces
1 (15-ounce) can garbanzo beans, rinsed and drained
1 (15-ounce) can kidney beans, rinsed and drained
1 (15-ounce) can white beans, rinsed and drained
1 (15-ounce) can black beans, rinsed and drained
1 ½ cups frozen lima beans
4 tablespoons cider vinegar
2 tablespoons honey
2 teaspoons dried oregano
5 tablespoons olive oil
Salt and pepper, to taste

Place all the beans in a large bowl. Toss gently to incorporate.

In a small bowl, whisk together the vinegar, honey, oregano, oil, and pinch each of salt and pepper. Pour the vinaigrette over the bean salad. Toss gently to incorporate and coat all the ingredients. Chill for at least an hour before serving.

*The Iroquois cultivated more than sixty different kinds of beans. Supermarket selections aren't as varied these days, but we hope you can find at least seven for this salad. An anthropologist working in the nineteen teens found Scarlet Runner, Cranberry, Purple Flageolet, Yellow Eye, Golden Wax, and others like Wampum, Wild Goose, and Southern Prolific Beans among the Iroquois, which you'll probably only find in heritage seed catalogs these days. The Iroquois ate beans fresh or dried them for use throughout the year in soups and in bread.*

# Marinated White Bean Salad

*4 servings*

 You can make your own mint vinegar by simply saving all your mint stems. Place them in a jar and cover with white vinegar; refrigerate.

**2 (15.5-ounce) cans white beans, rinsed and drained**
**1 small red onion, thinly sliced**
**¼ cup diced red bell pepper**
**¼ cup diced green bell pepper**
**1 tablespoon fresh mint, chopped**
**2 tablespoons fresh flat-leaf parsley, chopped**
**1 teaspoon finely chopped shallot**
**1 teaspoon sugar**
**3 tablespoons white vinegar or mint vinegar**
**4 tablespoons olive oil**
**Salt and pepper, to taste**

*Abbot Augustus Low commissioned this watercolor, around 1900, for labels on the maple vinegar he produced on his vast holdings near Long Lake. 71.170.2a*

Place the white beans, onion, bell peppers, mint, and parsley in a non-metallic bowl. Toss gently to combine.

In a small jar, combine the shallot, sugar, vinegar, oil, and a pinch each of salt and pepper. Tighten the lid and shake vigorously. Pour the vinaigrette over the white bean salad and toss gently to evenly coat all the ingredients. Cover with plastic wrap and refrigerate for at least 1 hour before serving to allow the flavors to develop.

*Adirondack homemakers commonly made their own vinegar from apple cider or maple sap. They could make a fine white vinegar, such as the one used in this recipe, by fermenting white sugar in water.*

# Slow-Cooked Beets with Greens and Goat Cheese

*8 servings*

**4 large red beets**
**I tablespoon olive oil**
**¹/₂ teaspoon kosher salt**
**¹/₂ teaspoon ground black pepper**
**4 sprigs fresh thyme**
**¹/₂ cup red wine**
**¹/₂ cup dark balsamic vinegar**
**2 tablespoons honey**
**8 ounces mixed baby greens**
**4 ounces goat cheese, crumbled**

Preheat oven to 350 degrees.

Place the beets in a deep glass baking dish. Add the oil and coat the beets evenly. Sprinkle the salt and pepper over the beets. Add the thyme sprigs, wine, and vinegar. Cover with aluminum foil and bake until the beets are tender, approximately 1–1¹/₂ hours.

Remove the beets from the baking dish and allow them to cool. Strain the liquid from the bottom of the dish into a small bowl. Add the honey to the liquid and whisk it to incorporate to make the dressing.

When the beets have cooled, peel them then thinly slice. Arrange the sliced beets on your serving plates or platter. Toss the greens in a bowl with the dressing and place some on each plate. Sprinkle the crumbled goat cheese as a finishing touch.

*Until late in the twentieth century, most Adirondack goats were novelties rather than milk-producers. This little boy hitched his rig to a goat in Conifer in the early twentieth century. P 4087*

# Field Greens with Maple Vinaigrette

*4 servings*

**12 ounces baby field greens (or mesclun mix)**
**1 cucumber, sliced**
**12 cherry tomatoes, cut in half**
**2 tablespoons pure maple syrup**
**1 tablespoon white vinegar**
**2 tablespoons vegetable oil**
**Salt and pepper, to taste**

Place the greens, cucumber, and tomatoes in a large bowl.

In a small bowl, whisk together the maple syrup, vinegar, oil, and a pinch each of salt and pepper. Pour the dressing over the greens, toss gently, and serve.

*You will probably find it most convenient to use mesclun mix in this salad, but it if you want a taste of the Adirondack fields as our ancestors did, go foraging. Jim Lillibridge, a farmer in the town of Thurman, typically gathered young "red root plants," probably pigweed, when he hoed his cornfield in the 1930s. You could also eat "dandylions," as did the Clarks of Cranberry Lake, or do as the Indians did and seek out wood sorrel and watercress to eat raw.*

*This recipe calls for white vinegar and maple syrup to evoke the taste of historic maple vinegar. If you sugar yourself, you can try making maple vinegar. It is a simple one-step process, the fermentation from sugar to alcohol to acetic acid happening in a natural progression. Directions for maple vinegar from the Hopkinton Maple Festival Cookbook specify using the last run of the sugaring season—probably because that sap makes inferior syrup. You add yeast to a barrel of partially boiled-down sap and set it in the sun. In March 1909, Lucelia Clark "done over some old sugar into vinegar" using this process.*

# Corn and Sweet Pea Salad

*4 servings*

**6 ears fresh corn on the cob**
**I cup green peas (fresh or frozen)**
**¹/₂ cup diced red bell pepper**
**¹/₄ cup diced red onion**
**¹/₂ cup sour cream**
**I teaspoon sugar**
**I tablespoon cider vinegar**
**I tablespoon chopped fresh dill**
**Salt and pepper, to taste**

Husk the corn and remove all the silk. Use a knife to remove the kernels from each cob. Place the corn kernels in a large bowl then add the peas, bell pepper, and onion.

In a small bowl, whisk together the sour cream, sugar, vinegar, dill, and a pinch each of salt and pepper. Add the dressing to the bowl with the corn salad mixture. Toss gently to incorporate all the ingredients. Serve well chilled.

*Even in villages, Adirondackers kept large gardens well into the twentieth century. P 2896*

*The Mohawk, the Abenaki, and the white settlers of the nineteenth-century Adirondacks commonly grew four different types of corn: flint corn (known to the Mohawk as "soup corn"), dent corn (starchier and used by them for bread), popcorn, and sweet corn. Some corn they ate green right after harvest. Most they husked and stored. The Mohawks peeled the husks back, braided them, and then hung the strings in their longhouses. The settlers husked the ears completely and stored them in a corncrib.*

*Adirondackers ate peas both fresh and dried. On August 3, 1910, Lucelia Clark wrote from her farm near Cranberry Lake, "We had green peas and new potatoes cooked together a real old fashioned dish."*

# Green Bean and Shaved Red Onion Salad

*4 servings*

**Salt and pepper, to taste**
**1 pound fresh green beans, trimmed**
**1 small red onion, thinly sliced**
**1½ tablespoons whole grain mustard**
**1 teaspoon sugar**
**1 tablespoon cider vinegar**
**3 tablespoons olive oil**

Fill a large bowl with ice water and set aside. Bring 2 quarts of water to boil with a pinch of salt. Add the green beans. Stir and cook for 1 minute. Remove from the boiling water and immediately place in the ice water. Chill thoroughly. Remove and drain.

Place the beans and onion in a large bowl. In a small jar, place the mustard, sugar, vinegar, oil, and a pinch each of salt and pepper. Close the lid tightly and shake vigorously. Pour the dressing over the beans and onions; toss gently to coat. Serve immediately.

*The gardening staff at Kamp Kill Kare, with its extensive greenhouses, didn't have to worry so much about the Adirondack climate as did other gardeners. This photo was taken about 1950. P 62097*

*Over the past century or so, we've gotten used to eating fresh green beans, pod and all. These modern beans have been bred for succulent pods. Before the flowering of scientific agriculture, the Iroquois didn't distinguish between their bean varieties with such precision, and ate many of their 60 plus varieties either fresh or dried.*

# Celery Root and Apple Slaw with Whole Grain Mustard and Horseradish

*4 Servings*

**1 tablespoon whole grain mustard**
**2 teaspoons prepared horseradish**
**⅓ cup mayonnaise**
**1 teaspoon fresh lemon juice**
**2 cups washed, peeled, and julienned celery root**
**¾ cup julienned Granny Smith apple**
**1 tablespoon chopped flat-leaf parsley**
**Salt and pepper, to taste**

Place the mustard, horseradish, mayonnaise, and lemon juice into a medium bowl and whisk together. Add the celery root, apple, and parsley. Toss together by hand until all the ingredients are incorporated. Adjust seasoning with salt and pepper. Refrigerate until ready to serve.

*Seneca Ray Stoddard, "The Old, Old Story:" love in an orchard, 1885. P 27686*

The celery root in this recipe is a modern introduction to Adirondack cuisine. If you wanted to experiment with a tuber that is little known now but was loved and cultivated by the Abenaki, substitute a Jerusalem artichoke for the celeriac. This slaw is a modern dish, as well. Classic slaw is a salad of raw cabbage that often graced Adirondack tables, from grand hotels to farmhouses. Apples are Adirondack staples, however, grown by the earliest settlers. You can still find apple trees growing at abandoned Adirondack homesites. Try the fruit; it might be some almost-forgotten cultivar like the Ben Davis, Wolfe Rivers, Pound Sweets, Gilly Flowers, Sheep-Noses, or Spice Sweetings that homesteaders planted in the Johnsburg area.

# Entrées

The concept of an entrée has evolved over the years. If you had
said "entrée" to an Adirondack farm wife a century ago, she would
have thought of a roasted joint of beef or a whole chicken around
which to build a meal. Guests at a great camp or grand hotel of
the time would have named several courses, including a fish course
coming before a meat course, which was likely to mean boiled beef
or a haunch of venison. Today, we are much more eclectic in what
we consider the centerpiece of a meal. In this section you will find
substantial stews such as might have graced the weekday table of a
hardworking farmer, joints, roasts, and fish dishes worthy of the bill
of fare at Camp Santanoni on Newcomb Lake or the Stevens House
in Lake Placid, and vegetarian dishes that a Victorian diner might
have looked askance at.

# Buckwheat Pancakes

*12 pancakes*

**2 cups buckwheat flour**
**4 teaspoons baking powder**
**¹/₂ teaspoon kosher salt**
**2 cups plus 1 tablespoon water**
**2 tablespoons vegetable oil**
**Butter**
**Maple Syrup**

In a large bowl, whisk together the flour, baking powder, and salt. Add the water and oil; whisk to mix.

Preheat pancake griddle until a drop of water "dances" on it. Use nonstick cooking spray or oil to coat griddle, as needed.

Spoon the batter onto hot griddle to make pancakes about 4–5 inches across. Turn when edges seem dry (they won't brown much because they don't contain sugar). Serve while hot with butter and maple syrup for a traditional breakfast.

*Like oats, buckwheat was widely grown because it can be used in many ways. It does well in a cool, moist climate, it quickly matures, and it can be eaten by man and beast. It is also a good crop for a pioneer farm because it is vigorous and can crowd out competing weeds in newly cultivated soil. Despite the name, buckwheat isn't wheat and doesn't have gluten so it tends to make a heavy bread. In the 1850s, Joel Tyler Headley reported that his guide, Bill Nye, made "... 'dog-chokers,' as the huge thick cakes, somewhat resembling pancakes, were called ..." which he served with venison. These were probably pure buckwheat pancakes. Daisy Dalaba Allen remembered buckwheat pancakes more fondly, writing that her family ate a lot of them in the Baker's Mills of the 1930s. Her mother's pancakes were a rich yellowish-brown, made with a little sour cream, freshly churned buttermilk, and baking soda.*

# Pan-Fried Trout and Caramelized Onions

*4 servings*

 As a general rule, whenever I am cooking fish with the skin on; I cook the skin side first to get it crispy. The skin of fish can be delicious, but it has to be crispy; nobody wants to eat soggy fish skin. Whenever I am serving fish with the skin on, I always serve it skin side up. This helps to keep the skin crispy and is immediately visible to whomever it is served to. They can then decide to eat the skin or not, with no surprises of finding the skin buried in the dish.

**4 trout, boned and filleted**
**Salt and pepper, to taste**
**¼ cup all-purpose flour**
**¼ cup cornmeal**
**5 tablespoons vegetable oil**
**2 tablespoons butter**
**2 cups peeled and julienned yellow onion**

Lay the trout fillets out flat on a plate or plastic wrap. Sprinkle both sides of each fillet with salt and pepper. In a pie tin, combine the flour and corn meal; dredge the fillets in the flour mixture.

Preheat the oil in a heavy sauté pan over medium-high heat. Carefully add half of the fillets to the hot pan. If you have left the skin on the fillets, cook the skin side first. Cook until golden brown, about 2 minutes, then turn over and repeat the process on the second side. Remove the trout from pan and drain on a plate lined with paper towels. Repeat the process to cook the other half of the fillets.

Heat the butter in a large heavy-bottom sauté pan over medium heat. Add the onions and turn the heat up to high. Cook the onions until they start to caramelize, stirring often to keep them from sticking too much. Caramelizing the onions will take about 10 minutes. Serve the onions over the hot pan-fried fillets.

Tourists enjoying the modest comforts of the small hotels and boarding houses counted venison and trout as much a part of their Adirondack experience as the fresh, bracing air and the lovely views. At many of these establishments, the cook would prepare your catch. Lucelia Clark, who lived on a small farm on the Windfall near Cranberry Lake, boarded and lodged tourists as a significant source of summer income. In 1908, with a houseful of guests, she wrote in her diary, "I have cooked trout until I am ashamed to look one in the face."

*Henry and Lucelia Clark on their farm near Cranberry Lake with a mess of fish destined for the table about 1915. P73385*

# Beaver Stew

*4 servings*

 I am not aware of any possibilities of buying beaver meat commercially. You either have to catch them yourself or make friends with a trapper who will share. Those in the know might be reluctant to give up such a tasty creature in favor of keeping the delectable meat for themselves. Sometimes beaver can be a hard sell to get people to try it, but I have never had someone try it and not like it.

**1 ½ pounds boneless beaver meat, cut into cubes**
**Salt and pepper, to taste**
**4 tablespoons vegetable oil**
**1 cup large-dice yellow onion**
**1 cup peeled and large-dice carrots**
**1 cup trimmed and large-dice celery**
**4 large red bliss potatoes, washed and quartered**
**3 tablespoons all-purpose flour**
**1 cup red wine**
**1 bay leaf**
**1 teaspoon chopped fresh thyme**
**1 teaspoon chopped fresh rosemary**
**1 quart beef broth or stock**

Season the beaver meat with salt and pepper. Heat a heavy-bottom stock pot over high heat. Add the oil then immediately add the meat. Stir with a wooden spoon periodically to sear the meat evenly on all sides. Once the meat is browned, add the onion, carrots, celery, and potatoes. Stir to coat with the oil in the pan. Cook for 3–4 minutes to get some color on the vegetables.

Turn the heat down to medium and add the flour. Stir until the flour absorbs all the oil and moisture in the pan. Add the wine, bay leaf, thyme, and rosemary; stir again to make a smooth paste, or roux, from the flour and the wine. Slowly add the broth, stirring constantly to prevent any lumps from forming. Turn the heat up and bring the mixture to a boil. Reduce heat to a simmer and cook until the meat and potatoes are tender, about 40 minutes. Stir occasionally while cooking. Adjust the seasoning with salt and pepper and serve while hot.

One of the earliest maps of the Adirondacks labels the central mountain area as the "Beaver Hunting Country of the Six Nations." In 1776, when the map was drawn, Iroquois trappers traded beaver pelts for iron kettles, woolen cloth, firearms, and beads at trading posts in the lowlands. The pelts were in high demand because makers of fashionable top hats valued beaver fur for its superior felting qualities. Indian trappers probably stewed the meat as in this recipe, and roasted the tail, which they particularly valued, in the embers of the fire.

*By the late nineteenth century when this photo was taken by Saranac Lake photographer William Kollecker, beaver had been almost extirpated in the Adirondacks and trappers sought animals like fox whose pelts would be used as furs. P41160*

# Lentil-Stuffed Yellow Squash

*4 servings*

**4 medium to large yellow squash**
**2 tablespoons olive oil**
**1 ¹/₂ cups cooked lentils**
**¹/₄ cup diced red onion**
**¹/₄ cup diced carrot**
**1 tablespoon cider vinegar**
**2 tablespoons vegetable oil**
**1 tablespoon chopped fresh tarragon**
**1 tablespoon chopped fresh chives**
**Salt and pepper, to taste**

Preheat oven to 375 degrees.

Wash the squash and pat them dry. Cut off both ends and use a hand held corer to remove the insides of all the squash. You may have to work your way in from both ends to get the entire soft seedy center out. Rub each of the squash inside and out with the olive oil.

In a large bowl, combine the lentils, onion, carrot, vinegar, vegetable oil, tarragon, chives, and a pinch each of salt and pepper. Mix to incorporate. Use your hands to firmly squeeze some of the mixture to smash it up a bit. This will help to hold the filling together after baking. Taste the mixture and adjust seasoning with salt and pepper, if necessary.

Stuff a quarter of the mixture into each of the hollowed out squash. Place on a baking sheet. Bake for 25–30 minutes, until the squash is tender and the filling is hot.

To plate the squash, slice a ¹/₂-inch wheel off each end of the squash then cut the middle piece in half on the bias. Stand the two large pieces up on the plate on the flat end, place the two wheels on the plate, and serve.

The Western Abenaki grew squashes along with corn, beans, Jerusalem artichokes, and tobacco. They favored river bottoms for their fields, not only because the land was good, but because it was close to spring fishing for another important food source. As with the Iroquois, care of the crops was the province of women, and the all-important job of scaring off the crows and other pests fell to the children.

This image by photographer Seneca Ray Stoddard may be part of a story. In the companion image, the little boy is asleep among the squash. P 30448

# Baked Stuffed Acorn Squash

*4 servings*

**2 large acorn squash**
**4 tablespoons olive oil, divided**
**Salt and pepper, to taste**
**2 cups cooked wild rice**
**1/2 cup diced yellow onion**
**1/2 cup diced celery**
**1/4 cup chopped dried apple**
**1/4 cup dried cranberries**
**1/2 cup shelled hazelnuts, toasted and crushed**
**2 tablespoons chopped fresh chives**
**1 tablespoon cider vinegar**

Preheat oven to 350 degrees.

Wash the acorn squash and pat dry. Cut the squash in half and scoop out and discard the seeds. Rub the squash inside and out with 2 tablespoons oil and sprinkle with salt and pepper. Place the squash halves in a baking dish.

In a large bowl, combine the rice, onion, celery, apple, cranberries, hazelnuts, chives, vinegar, remaining oil, and a pinch each of salt and pepper. Stir to mix all the ingredients thoroughly. Taste the filling and adjust seasoning, if necessary.

Place a quarter of the mixture into each of the squash. Bake until the squash is tender and the filling is hot, about 45–50 minutes.

*The Iroquois ate squash year around, by itself and along with other foods, at home and on the trail. Iroquois hunters traveling to the Adirondacks in the fall took dried strips of pumpkin which they chewed along the way; in the winter, in their villages in the Mohawk valley, they kept squash fresh in bark-lined pits. They boiled squash in kettles, baked it in the ashes, cooked it with beans, and mixed mashed, cooked squash in with ground corn to make bread. In making this dish, you are carrying on a culinary tradition that goes back thousands of years to the Iroquois longhouse where women boiled cranberry beans and served them in roasted squash shells.*

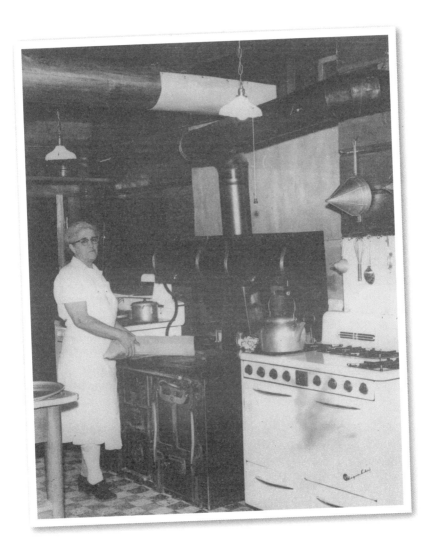

*The cook at great Camp Uncas in 1950
had several ways to bake her squash.
In between her two modern gas ranges
sits the old standby, a wood cookstove.
P 41043*

# Skillet-Cooked Grouse

*4 servings*

 Grouse are a delicious game bird. While small in size, the effort put into pursuing and cleaning these birds is well worth the trouble. Aside from seeing some beautiful countryside in pursuit of harvesting the birds, the delicate meat of a game bird feeding exclusively on wild nuts and seeds is unparalleled.

**2 grouse, plucked clean**
**2 tablespoons olive oil**
**2 cloves garlic, chopped**
**1 teaspoon chopped fresh thyme**
**1 teaspoon chopped fresh rosemary**
**Salt and pepper, to taste**

Preheat oven to 350 degrees.

Place the grouse breast side down on a cutting board. Use kitchen shears to cut along both sides of the backbone. Remove and discard the backbone. Use a boning knife to remove the rib cage from each side. Then use the tip of the knife to carefully remove the keel bone, being careful not to cut through the breast meat or skin.

Coat each flattened out, semi-boneless bird, inside and out, with oil. Sprinkle each bird with half of the garlic, thyme, rosemary, and a pinch each of salt and pepper.

Heat a cast iron skillet over medium-high heat. Place the birds skin side down in the hot skillet. Cook until the skin is golden brown and crispy, about 5 minutes. Turn the birds over. Place the skillet in oven and cook for about 10 minutes. When the grouse is done, the juices will come out clear.

Cut the birds in half following the seam where the keel bone was, separating the two breasts. Each portion will include a breast with only the wing bone attached and a leg with the thigh bone and drumstick attached. Serve hot, skin side up.

Samuel H. Hammond heard a ruffed grouse, or partridge (as it is known in the Adirondacks), when he visited in the late 1850s. "Hark! To that dull sound, like blows upon some soft, hollow, half sonorous substance, slow and measured at first, but increasing in rapidity, until it rolls like the beat of a muffled drum, or the low growl of the far-off thunder. It is the partridge drumming upon his log." Hammond enjoyed eating the bird broiled over the campfire.

*The gentleman on the left and his friend (taking the picture) have engaged two guides for their Adirondack camping trip. One guide is tending the fire, perhaps getting ready to broil some partridges, while the other, axe in hand, is collecting firewood or putting the finishing touches on the bark-roofed lean-to near New Russia, 1884. P7651*

# Wild Turkey Burger with Dill Mayonnaise

*4 servings*

 Wild turkeys are built very different than their domesticated counterparts. The breasts are not as developed; otherwise the extra weight would keep them from being able to fly. They spend most of their time on the ground looking for food. When in danger, they are more likely to run first, using flight as a last resort. This leaves the legs of a wild turkey very lean and somewhat tough. Grinding is an excellent way to utilize this meat and make it more palatable.

**1 ½ pounds ground wild turkey**
**2 cloves garlic, chopped**
**2 leaves fresh basil, chopped**
**Salt and pepper, to taste**
**½ cup mayonnaise**
**1 teaspoon freshly squeezed lemon juice**
**1 tablespoon chopped fresh dill**
**4 Kaiser rolls**
**4 pieces romaine lettuce**
**4 slices tomato**

Place the ground turkey, garlic, basil, and a pinch each of salt and pepper in a large bowl. Use your hands to mix the ingredients all together. Divide the meat into 4 equal balls. Press each ball into a patty.

Cook the patties on a preheated grill (charcoal or wood coals are best). The turkey burgers are done when the juices come out clear.

In small bowl, combine the mayonnaise, lemon juice, dill, and a pinch each of salt and pepper. Whisk together.

Spread a small amount of the dill mayo on both the top and bottom portion of the rolls. Place a turkey burger on the bottom half of each roll. Top with lettuce and tomato and enjoy.

Although wild turkeys were absent from the Adirondacks for a century, farmers often kept their domesticated cousins. Julia Baker Kellogg raised them on her farm near Minerva as a source of income. On November 19, 1886, she plucked and dressed eight turkeys. "Took me all day," she wrote in her diary. The next day she packed them in barrels and sent them off with her husband to market, just in time for Thanksgiving. As a national holiday, Thanksgiving was only a generation old at the time. Largely due to the efforts of Godey's Lady's Book editor Sarah Josepha Hale, Thanksgiving had been established by President Lincoln in 1863.

Adirondack farm families might grow fond of their animals, but even the youngest children, like Bernice Bostock and Amos Hough, knew that the animals, like this turkey, were destined for the table. Photo taken about 1910. P 18823

# Wild Turkey Roulade

*6–8 servings*

 The beauty of this dish is that it utilizes the whole turkey. Wild turkeys are different enough from their domestic counterparts that they do not lend themselves as well to the whole roasted bird that we are accustomed to on holidays. The grinding of the leg meat and the pounding of the breast meat make for a much more tender finished product, a better use for a wild bird.

**I skin-on, boneless wild turkey breast**
**I ½ pounds ground wild turkey**
**4 teaspoons ground fennel seeds**
**2 teaspoons ground coriander seeds**
**I teaspoon red pepper flakes**
**I teaspoon celery seeds**
**2 teaspoons chopped fresh rosemary**
**2 teaspoons chopped fresh thyme**
**I teaspoon ground black pepper**
**2 teaspoons kosher salt**
**Salt and pepper, to taste**
**2 tablespoons olive oil**

Preheat oven to 350 degrees.

Place the turkey breast on a large cutting board, skin side down. Use a knife to make an incision from the thick end of the breast, toward the thinner section. Do not remove this piece of meat, rather make a flap and fold it over. We are looking to make the breast the same thickness all the way across. Use a meat mallet to pound the meat into a rectangle about ¾ inch thick. Cover with plastic wrap and refrigerate until needed later.

In a large bowl, combine the ground turkey, fennel, coriander, pepper flakes, celery seeds, rosemary, thyme, ground pepper, and kosher salt. Use your hands to thoroughly mix all the ingredients together.

Lay out 2 (18-inch) lengths of aluminum foil so that they overlap 3–4 inches in the middle. Place the turkey breast, skin side down in the middle of the foil. Sprinkle a pinch each of salt and pepper over the breast. Use your hands to form the ground meat sausage into a log the

*Photographer H. M. Beach's picture of "Turkey Day in Lisbon" was taken in a village just to the north of the Adirondacks about 1910. The turkeys are domestic ones. P 2214*

length of the turkey breast. Place the sausage on the breast and wrap the meat around the sausage.

Drizzle the oil over the roulade and sprinkle with another pinch each of salt and pepper on the skin side of the roulade. Roll the roulade up into the foil as tightly as possible. Twist the ends tight to help keep the roulade together and to trap the juices. Place on a baking sheet and bake until the internal temperature reaches 165 degrees—check temperature after 45 minutes cooking time. Remove from the oven and allow to rest for 10 minutes.

Remove the roulade from the foil. Heat a large cast iron skillet over medium-high heat. Add a small amount of oil then place in the skillet. Brown the outside to get the skin crispy, rolling occasionally to brown all sides. Remove from the skillet. Slice and serve while hot.

# Slow-Roasted Duck with Cherries

*4 servings*

 In this recipe, I used a store-bought, large farm-raised duck. The reason is two-fold. First, domestic ducks are large enough to serve 4 people. Secondly, most states do not recommend eating the skin from wild ducks. This would not have been an issue hundreds of years ago, but in this day and age, if a duck eats any contaminates from pollution along the migration route, it is most often stored in the fatty tissue. Wild ducks are great to eat, it is just recommended to skin them first which does not lend them to whole roasting.

**1 (5–6 pound) whole duck**
**1 teaspoon ground coriander**
**$1/2$ teaspoon ground ginger**
**1 teaspoon kosher salt**
**1 teaspoon ground black pepper**
**1 cup red wine**
**1 cup pitted fresh dark cherries**
**2 tablespoons honey**
**Salt and pepper, to taste**

Preheat oven to 350 degrees. Trim the excess fat from around the neck and tail area of the duck and discard. Use the tip of a knife to score the skin on the breast. This will allow the fat to render during roasting.

In a small bowl, combine the coriander, ginger, salt, and pepper. Mix thoroughly. Sprinkle the mixture all over the duck, being sure to cover the breast and legs specifically.

Place the duck, breast up, in a roasting pan and place in oven. Roast for 1–1$1/2$ hours, using a meat thermometer to check the internal temperature. Remove the duck from the oven when the internal temperature reaches 155 degrees. Let rest for 10 minutes before carving.

While the duck is cooking, make the cherry sauce. In a medium saucepan, place the wine, cherries, honey, and a pinch each of salt and pepper. Bring to boil and cook over high heat until the liquid reduces by half, about 15 minutes.

Carve the meat from the duck, spoon the sauce over the meat, and serve while hot.

For the past century and a half, at least, cooks have thought of "roasting" as something done in an enclosed oven. When Yankee farmers began settling the Adirondacks, however, the oven was a fairly new invention, and many regretted the end of home roasting in front of an open fire. Hunters and tourists who camped out in the nineteenth century could recreate the meat-cooking method of their grandmothers. Some of them used a reflector oven to concentrate the heat from their campfire; others spitted the meat or hung it on a string so it could turn and cook evenly.

You can use domesticated cherries for this dish, or, for a real taste of history, do as the Clark family did on September 22, 1912. "We all went up on the plains and gathered black cherries and ate until we could not swallow anymore," wrote Mrs. Clark in her diary.

Nelson Patnode waited for ducks in a rock blind on Chazy Lake in the 1930s. Patnode's hunting and fishing helped feed his family during the Depression. P 68438

# Forest Mushroom and Goose Sausage

*4 servings*

 Goose meat with the skin removed can be dry when cooked, that is why I put a little ground pork in the sausage. The fat provides the moisture and mouth feel that people associate with sausage. I chose lobster, morel, and chanterelle mushrooms for this dish because they all grow in the wild throughout the Adirondacks.

**1 pound ground goose meat**
**¼ pound ground pork**
**2 teaspoons ground fennel seeds**
**1 teaspoon ground coriander**
**½ teaspoon celery seeds**
**1 teaspoon kosher salt**
**1 teaspoon ground black pepper**
**2 tablespoons olive oil**
**2 cloves garlic, chopped**
**2 tablespoons chopped shallots**
**2 ounces fresh lobster mushrooms, cleaned**
**2 ounces fresh morel mushrooms, cleaned**
**2 ounces fresh chanterelle mushrooms, cleaned**
**Salt and pepper, to taste**

In a large bowl, combine the goose meat, pork, fennel, coriander, celery seeds, kosher salt, and ground black pepper. Mix the ingredients thoroughly, cover, and refrigerate.

Heat the oil in a large sauté pan over medium-high heat. Add the garlic and shallots. Stir with a wooden spoon, cooking until the mixture just starts to brown.

Roughly chop all the mushrooms; add them to the sauté pan. Sprinkle with salt and pepper. Cook over medium heat until the mushrooms are tender, about 10 minutes. Remove the mushrooms from the heat, place in a separate dish, and refrigerate until well chilled.

Add the mushroom mixture to the ground meat mixture. Use your hands to thoroughly mix all the ingredients. At this point you have bulk sausage that can be used as is in a variety of other recipes including meaty pasta sauces, soups, etc. You can also form the sausage into patties and grill until they reach an internal temperature of 155 degrees and serve with your favorite condiments. If you have the equipment, you can stuff the sausage into hog casings and make sausage links that can be grilled or cooked in pasta sauce.

*Experienced mycologists will have fun finding the mushrooms for this sausage. Chicken of the woods, morels, puffballs, chanterelles, and lobster mushrooms all grow in the cool, moist, Adirondack woods. Adirondack white settlers may not have been terribly keen on mushrooms—no references to gathering them survive—but the Indians used mushrooms in soup or fried them in grease. Beware if you eat puffballs; the Iroquois believed that it would make you jealous.*

*Martha Reben and Fred Rice were probably not about to eat this Canada goose they met about 1960. Reben was an avid observer of nature who spent ten summers camping out and recovering from tuberculosis on Weller Pond. Fred Rice was her guide. Reben wrote three books which remain Adirondack classics about her experiences. P 47524*

# Pork Chops and Applesauce

*4 servings*

**4 (6-ounce) boneless pork loin chops**
**1 teaspoon chopped fresh rosemary**
**Salt and pepper, to taste**
**2 tablespoons vegetable oil**
**4 cups peeled and diced Granny Smith apples**
**1 cup apple juice**
**1/2 cup light brown sugar**
**1 teaspoon ground cinnamon**

Sprinkle the pork chops evenly with the rosemary, salt, and pepper.
Drizzle with oil and evenly coat. Cover and refrigerate while making
the applesauce.

In a large saucepan, combine the apples, juice, brown sugar, and
cinnamon. Bring to a boil, reduce the heat to a simmer, and cook until
the apples are very soft and the juice has reduced, about 45 minutes.
Remove from the heat and let stand for 10 minutes. Use an immersion
blender to purée the mixture until smooth. Return to the stove and
keep warm until ready to serve.

Preheat oven to 350 degrees.

Heat a cast iron skillet over medium-high heat. Add the pork chops
and sear until golden brown. Turn the pork chops over and place
the skillet in oven. Cook for about 10 minutes. Check the internal
temperature of the pork chops with a meat thermometer, and when
the temperature reaches 155 degrees, remove the skillet from the
oven. Allow the chops to rest for 5 minutes before serving with the
warm applesauce.

Pigs were ideal animals for Adirondackers, homesteaders, and gentleman farmers alike. Swine ranged free around the little farms, rooting for beechnuts and other wild food, and also consumed buttermilk or any other leftovers from the house. Great camp pig management was often more systematic. Robert C. Pruyn seriously studied scientific agriculture and kept registered Black Berkshire pigs in a model piggery at Camp Santanoni on Newcomb Lake. His staff butchered and cured pork on the farm and yearly sent 50 hams and 100 sides of bacon to the Pruyns' town house in Albany around the turn of the last century.

Surgeon Arpad Gerster served his guests a combination of local foods and sophisticated delicacies when they visited his Camp Oteetiwi on Raquette Lake. The sorrel for the soup was gathered in the woods, the fish caught right outside the door, and the "Murphies" served with it were locally-grown Irish potatoes. The centerpiece of the meal, the roast pig, was raised by one of his neighbors. The Roquefort cheese and the wines came from dealers in New York. 1958.273.0016

# Sausage Polenta-Stuffed Roast Pork Loin

*6–8 servings*

**3 pounds boneless pork loin**
**Salt and pepper, to taste**
**1/2 pound Italian sausage**
**1/8 teaspoon cayenne pepper**
**I tablespoon chopped fresh rosemary**
**5 cloves roasted garlic***
**I teaspoon sugar**
**1 1/2 cups heavy cream**
**1 1/2 cups milk**
**I cup cornmeal**

Cut the pork loin in a book-fold fashion so that it folds out into a rectangle. Pound the meat with a meat mallet on both sides. Season both sides with salt and pepper. Cover and refrigerate until ready to stuff.

In a large heavy-bottom saucepan, crumble the sausage and cook over medium heat until just done. Add the cayenne, rosemary, garlic, sugar, and a pinch each of salt and pepper. Stir briefly to incorporate all ingredients. Once the sausage is cooked, drain off excess fat.

Add in the cream and milk. Bring to a boil and immediately reduce to a simmer. Allow to simmer for 10 minutes. Slowly whisk in the cornmeal—the mixture should still be fairly thin and a pale yellow color. Continue to whisk over low heat until the mixture becomes thick. Remove the whisk and continue to stir with a wooden spoon. When it's creamy and smooth and the cornmeal has lost some its grainy texture, it's done. Spread the polenta out onto a baking sheet with sides and allow to cool.

When polenta is cool, form it roughly into a log shape. Place the pork loin so that the fat side is facing down with the fatty portion furthest away from you. Place the polenta log about 1 inch from the edge closest to you. Roll the polenta up inside the pork. When you're finished rolling, the fatty side of the pork should be on the outside. Tie with string in about 5 places to hold it together.

Preheat oven to 350 degrees. Sear the pork roll in a hot cast iron skillet to get some color on the meat and start the process of rendering the fat. Place in oven until it reaches an internal temperature of 155 degrees. Remove from oven and allow to rest at room temperature for at least 10 minutes. Cut off the strings and slice the pork roast into ¹/₂-inch slices.

\* To roast garlic, place an entire bulb of garlic in aluminum foil and drizzle with olive oil and salt and pepper. Place into a 350-degree oven and roast until soft and golden, approximately 25 minutes. The garlic can then be squeezed out.

> *Adirondack farmers slaughtered their hogs in the fall when the weather became cold enough that the meat wouldn't spoil too quickly. It was only then that the family ate fresh pork. Adirondack settlers preserved the rest and, with luck, ate it all winter. Many farm wives, like Ida Beldin Parker of Newcomb, pickled the fatback, leaving it in the brine and fishing it out as she needed it. Hams and bacon could be pickled in brine and then smoked, or rubbed with a dry solution of salt, spices, and sugar before smoking. The Clark family near Cranberry Lake butchered several hogs each fall. Mrs. Clark "took care of the meat," preserving everything but the squeal, as she might have said. On November 24, 1916, she had unwelcome help. "I tried lard & made head cheese," she wrote. "Collie stole a couple of pork cheeks. She has plenty of cheek!"*

*These four pigs lived at Twitchell Lake in the 1920s. P 61756*

# Mushroom-Stuffed Braised Veal Breast

*6–8 servings*

**3 pounds boneless veal breast**
**Salt and pepper, to taste**
**3 tablespoons olive oil**
**1 tablespoon chopped garlic**
**1 tablespoon chopped shallot**
**3 cups sliced mushrooms (button or cremini)**
**1 teaspoon chopped fresh thyme**
**1 teaspoon chopped fresh rosemary**
**3 tablespoons vegetable oil**
**3 carrots, peeled and large diced**
**3 celery stalks, large diced**
**1 yellow onion, peeled and large diced**
**2 cups red wine**
**1 quart beef broth**

Cut the veal in a book-fold fashion so that it folds out into a rectangle. Pound the meat with a meat mallet on both sides. Season both sides with salt and pepper. Cover and refrigerate until ready to stuff.

Heat the olive oil over medium heat in a large sauté pan. Add the garlic and shallot; cook until they just start to get some color on them. Add the mushrooms. Stir and sauté for several minutes until the mushrooms cook down and are soft. Add the thyme, rosemary, and a pinch each of salt and pepper. Stir to incorporate. Transfer the mushrooms to a shallow pan and refrigerate to cool.

Preheat oven to 325 degrees.

Lay out the veal and spread the mushrooms over it. Roll the veal breast up; trying to keep all the mushrooms inside as you roll. Tie the veal roll with butcher's twine about every $1^1/2$ inches to keep the roll together.

Heat a roasting pan over high heat. Add the vegetable oil then add the veal roll. Sear on all sides to get a nice golden brown color. Reduce the heat then add the carrots, celery, and onion to the pan. Stir. Add the wine and cook until the wine is reduced by half, about 10 minutes. Stir in the beef broth.

Place the roasting pan in the oven and cook for 45 minutes. Turn the veal roll over and cook for another 45 minutes. Remove from the oven and let rest for 10 minutes before removing the strings. Slice and serve while hot with some of the braising liquid and vegetables.

*Today, veal is a pricey, specialty meat. For a small, traditional farmer, it was common—just a by-product of the business. Adirondackers usually kept a cow or two for milk, and they had to breed her yearly to make her produce. They hoped for a female calf so they could add to the dairy herd. A male was of no use at all, unless they were going to castrate it and use the ox as a beast of burden, but by the late nineteenth century most farmers preferred horses. A little bull goes a long way, and usually there was only one in the neighborhood. Most young male cattle wound up on the table. Lucelia and Henry Clark let the doomed "vealers" feed from their mothers longer than their sisters in order to get milk-fed veal. In June of 1910, the Clarks butchered four vealers in one week.*

*In this view of the Clark house at Maple Grove Farm near Cranberry Lake taken about 1910, you can see the covered well in the right foreground next to the balsam tree. This was the Clark's cold storage, and one day Lucelia dropped a pail full of veal down the well when attempting to retrieve the meat for dinner. P73456*

# Stewed Chicken with Vegetables

*4 servings*

**4 chicken drumsticks**
**4 chicken thighs**
**Salt and pepper, to taste**
**2 tablespoons vegetable oil**
**6 cloves garlic, peeled**
**1 yellow onion, peeled and diced**
**2 carrots, peeled and large diced**
**2 celery stalks, large diced**
**¾ cup peeled and large diced celery root**
**¾ cup peeled and large diced turnip**
**1 tablespoon dried oregano**
**1 bay leaf**
**1 cup white wine**
**1 quart chicken broth or stock**

Preheat oven to 325 degrees.

Heat a large cast iron skillet or Dutch oven over high heat. Season the chicken pieces with salt and pepper. Add the oil to the pan then add the chicken and sear on all sides to evenly brown.

Add the garlic, onion, carrots, celery, celery root, turnip, oregano, and bay leaf. Stir to incorporate. Add the wine and cook for 3–4 minutes over high heat to reduce the wine by half. Add the chicken broth and a pinch each of salt and pepper. Bring to a boil then shut off heat.

Move the pan to the oven and cook, uncovered, until the chicken is "falling from the bone" tender, about 1hour. Serve 1 drumstick and 1 thigh per person with a helping of the vegetables and sauce.

*Adirondack farmers ate plenty of stewed chicken because stewing is a good way to tenderize an old, stringy hen or a rooster. A barnyard only needs one rooster so, like male cattle, male fowl were headed for the pot. Hens were dual-purpose animals—when they had outlived their usefulness as egg layers they, too, were eaten. Livonia Stanton Emerson, who moved to Long Lake as a four-year-old in 1849, remembered her mother's method of killing her fowl when it was time for a chicken dinner. She wrote, "It was not long after we moved into this wilderness before father brought mother a very nice rifle . . . . I can almost see her taking aim at her chickens, or geese, as they came up from the lake to the old log barn, one after the other, regular Indian file. It was bang, and off went their heads . . . ."*

George Bacon Wood, "Old Barn and Chickens," ca. 1886. P 20879

# Wild Turkey Pot Pie

*6 servings*

Making pie crust with lard is very traditional and yields a truly flaky crust. It is important that all the ingredients are cold in the preparation to maximize the flakiness of the finished product. If the dough gets overworked, it will reduce the flakiness and make the crust dense and tough.

## Filling

**1 pound boneless, skinless wild turkey**
**Salt and pepper, to taste**
**2 tablespoons butter**
**1 tablespoon olive oil**
**¾ cup diced yellow onion**
**¾ cup diced carrot**
**½ cup diced celery**
**6 ounces button mushrooms, quartered**
**1 teaspoon chopped fresh thyme**
**1 teaspoon chopped fresh rosemary**
**1 tablespoon chopped parsley**
**2 tablespoons all-purpose flour**
**1¾ cups turkey broth**
**¼ cup frozen peas, thawed**

## Pie Crust

**2 cups all-purpose flour**
**½ teaspoon kosher salt**
**⅔ cup lard, chilled**
**4 to 5 tablespoons ice water, or more as needed**
**1 egg, beaten**

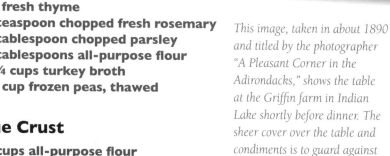

*This image, taken in about 1890 and titled by the photographer "A Pleasant Corner in the Adirondacks," shows the table at the Griffin farm in Indian Lake shortly before dinner. The sheer cover over the table and condiments is to guard against flies; there are no screens on the window and the barnyard is near. P 641*

**Filling:** Cut turkey into ½-inch dice and season with salt and pepper. Heat a large skillet over medium-high heat. Add the butter and oil. When the butter has melted, add the turkey. Cook for 3–4 minutes. Add the onion, carrot, celery, mushrooms, thyme, rosemary, and parsley. Stir to incorporate all ingredients. Cook for 5–6 minutes until the vegetables start to soften.

Add the flour and stir to incorporate. Add the broth and bring to a boil, stirring often. Reduce heat and simmer for 10–15 minutes. The flour should thicken the broth to make a gravy. Adjust the thickness with more flour, if necessary. Adjust seasoning with salt and pepper. Stir in the peas. Remove from heat, transfer to another container, and refrigerate to chill.

**Crust:** Sift the flour into a large bowl; add salt. Refrigerate until well chilled, about 15 minutes. Cut the lard into the flour using a pastry cutter or fork. Add the water, 1 tablespoon at a time, using the pastry cutter until it starts to form a dough. Work the dough into a ball, kneading 3–4 times, but do not overwork. Cover and refrigerate for $1/2$ hour. Cut the dough in half, and working on a floured surface, roll each piece into a circle slightly larger than a 9-inch pie pan.

Preheat oven to 400 degrees, place 1 crust in the bottom of a 9-inch glass pie pan, and fill with the turkey mixture.

Brush the edge of the pie dough with some beaten egg. Place the second crust on top. Use your fingers or a fork to crimp the edges together all the way around the pan. Brush the top with the remaining egg. Cut 6 evenly spaced $1/2$-inch-long slits into the dough. This allows steam to escape during cooking and helps mark the crust for serving.

Place the pot pie on a baking sheet and put into the oven. Bake for 30–35 minutes until the crust is golden brown and the filling is bubbling. Remove from the oven and let rest for 10 minutes before serving.

*"Mother was in the pantry, setting the top crust on the Sunday chicken pie. Three fat hens were in the pie, under the bubbling gravy. Mother spread the crust and crimped the edges, and the gravy showed through the two pine-trees she had cut in the dough."* So goes a passage familiar to readers of Farmer Boy, *the story of Almanzo Wilder's childhood near Malone, on the north slopes of the Adirondacks, in the 1860s. Chicken pies were standard Sunday and holiday dishes.*

# Seared Venison Loin with Blackberry Reduction Sauce

*4 Servings*

In cooking, I prefer to use table wine. There are "cooking wines" available for sale in some places, but I have never found one that did any justice to my cooking. My philosophy is that if it's not worth drinking then it's probably not worth cooking with.

## Venison

**½ (750-milliliter) bottle red wine**
**2 shallots, peeled and thinly sliced**
**4 cloves garlic, peeled and roughly chopped**
**8 sprigs fresh thyme**
**3 sprigs fresh rosemary**
**4 (6-ounce) portions venison loin**
**Salt and pepper, to taste**
**Olive oil**

*Seneca Ray Stoddard took this image of city sportsmen and their guides reliving the day's hunt in 1888. P 1678*

## Blackberry Reduction Sauce

**1 shallot, peeled and finely chopped**
**1 teaspoon olive oil**
**2 pints fresh blackberries**
**¼ cup sugar**
**½ (750-milliliter) bottle red wine**
**Salt and pepper, to taste**

**Venison:** Pour the wine into a large bowl. Add the shallots and garlic. Pick the thyme and rosemary leaves from the stems, add them to the bowl, and gently stir. Place the venison pieces in the bowl and roll them around a bit to cover all sides with the marinade. Cover with plastic wrap and refrigerate overnight.

When it's time to cook, preheat the oven to 350 degrees and remove the venison from the marinade and pat dry with a paper towel. Season each piece with salt and pepper and lightly coat with oil.

Sear in a hot cast iron skillet on all sides. When searing is completed, place the skillet in the oven until preferred temperature is reached. Venison is best served medium rare, and cooking times will vary depending on the thickness of your particular cut of meat. Once the venison comes out of the oven, allow it to rest on a cutting board for 3–5 minutes before slicing and serving.

**Blackberry Reduction Sauce:**  In a small saucepan, sweat the shallot in oil. Add the blackberries and sugar, stirring with a wooden spoon. Add the wine, stir again, and turn the heat up to bring it to a boil.

Once it comes to a boil, reduce the heat slightly and allow the sauce to simmer for quite some time. Reduce the sauce enough that the wine starts to thicken. Remove from the heat and adjust seasoning with salt and pepper, to taste. Serve drizzled over the venison.

*The quintessential taste of the Adirondacks is venison and has been since the days of the Iroquois and Algonquin. As Yankee and French Canadian loggers began coming to the region in the mid-nineteenth century, the deer population boomed as axes and saws opened up thousands of acres to sunlight which encouraged the woody browse that deer thrive on. Venison was there for the taking and sustained many a homesteading family and lumber camp crew. It was also a source of income. "City men" paid locals to guide them on hunting expeditions, and local men could sell venison to hotels.*

*In 1854, James Wardner and two partners spent the winter hunting near Osgood Pond. They hung the "saddles" (loin, the choicest cut) in a shed to freeze, and jerked the rest of the meat. In March, they hauled six tons of dried and frozen meat to Port Kent, where they sold it to the Lake Champlain Transportation Company to serve on its lake steamboats.*

# Balsamic-Braised Rabbit with Morels

*4 servings*

 This dish is a fabulous example of a "one-pot meal." It is also a dish that closely resembles what Adirondackers prepared over a fire or on their woodstove, with a few modern additions made here for embellishment purposes.

**2 whole rabbits broken down into shoulders, legs, and loins**
**Salt and pepper, to taste**
**Olive oil**
**8 cloves garlic, peeled**
**1 medium yellow onion, large diced**
**2 carrots, peeled and large diced**
**8 red bliss potatoes**
**2 ounces dried morel mushrooms**
**6 sprigs fresh thyme**
**3 sprigs fresh rosemary**
**1/2 (750-milliliter) bottle red wine**
**1/2 cup dark balsamic vinegar**
**1 quart reduced veal stock**
**3/4 cup heavy cream**

Season the rabbit with salt and pepper and lightly coat with oil. Sear in a hot cast iron skillet to get a nice brown color on both sides.

Add the garlic, onion, and carrots. Cook over moderately high heat to get some color on the vegetables then add the potatoes, mushrooms, thyme, and rosemary. Cook for approximately 1 minute. Add the wine, using it to deglaze the pan. Stir in the vinegar and stock. Bring to a boil then reduce to a simmer.

Cook over low heat until the rabbit and vegetables are tender, approximately 1 hour. Add the cream and stir to incorporate. Adjust seasoning with salt and pepper, if necessary.

Hunting rabbits and hares with dogs is an old Adirondack sport, and the experience of being outdoors with the hounds is as important as the meat for the pot. Willet Randall, who bred the famous Patch line of beagles near North River in the first half of the twentieth century, delighted in being "out with the hounds, sitting in the front seat of my wildwood amphitheater high above the bowels of the big swamp where a panorama of enchanting beauty meets my gaze on every side," listening for the "flute-like notes and the bell-toned voices" of his dogs on the trail of a snowshoe hare.

Postcard view of "A Day's Sport at Stony Creek Inn" about 1940. 2004.12.13

# Bacon-Wrapped Trout

*4 servings*

**4 slices fresh lemon**
**4 sprigs fresh thyme**
**4 whole trout, cleaned**
**Salt and pepper, to taste**
**8 slices bacon**

Preheat oven to 350 degrees.

Place a slice of lemon and a sprig of thyme inside of each trout. Sprinkle each one, inside and out, with a small amount of salt and pepper and wrap with 2 strips of bacon, working from the head back.

Heat a large cast iron skillet over medium heat. Add the trout and cook until the bacon starts to get crispy, about 6–8 minutes. Turn the trout then place the skillet into oven. Cook for 10–12 minutes. When done, the bacon should be crispy all the way around and the flesh of the fish will flake off and be opaque white.

*This guest at Brandreth Park, a private estate west of Long Lake, caught a nice mess of brook trout in 1890. P 61090*

*Adirondack Murray's best-selling Adventures in the Wilderness started a tourist boom after the Civil War. He decreed that "coffee, tea, sugar, pepper, pork, and condensed milk . . . are all you need to carry in with you." The pork was for cooking grease—the fattier the better—and also contributed salt. Murray felt that you needn't carry anything else because you would subsist on the bounty of the woods—trout and venison primarily. We've substituted bacon for salt pork in this dish.*

# Rosemary and Sea Salt Crispy-Skinned Turkey Breast

*4 servings*

When I first saw a turkey breast prepared in this fashion, I thought the gentleman was crazy. That was until I tried the finished product! It may be the nostalgia of eating something hot off the fire like a camper may have done long ago or it may be the residual ash left on the meat while cooking, but either way it's simply delicious. While not the same, similar results can be obtained by cooking the turkey in a hot cast iron skillet.

**1 ½ pounds boneless wild turkey breast, skin on**
**1 tablespoon coarse sea salt**
**1 teaspoon coarse-ground black pepper**
**2 teaspoons chopped fresh rosemary**
**2 tablespoons vegetable oil**

Preheat a 3-inch bed of hardwood coals.

Sprinkle the turkey with salt, pepper, and rosemary. Drizzle the oil onto the breast and rub it in to evenly coat.

Place the turkey directly on the coals and cook for 12–15 minutes. Turn the breast over and cook for an additional 5 minutes. Remove from the coals and brush any excess ash from the turkey. Allow to rest for 10 minutes, slice, and serve while hot.

*Sea salt has become popular lately with the availability of modern cheap transportation and our awareness of what were once exotic foods. Until about 1900, Adirondackers, like most everyone else in the northeastern United States, used salt from the famous salt works in Syracuse. Syracuse salt was refined from brine that came from underground.*

# Sautéed Trout with Potatoes, Parsnips, and Lemon Brown Butter

*4 Servings*

## Potatoes

8 red bliss potatoes, washed
Salt and pepper, to taste
2 teaspoons chopped fresh thyme
2 teaspoons chopped fresh rosemary
2 tablespoons melted butter
2 tablespoons olive oil

## Parsnips

2 large parsnips, washed, peeled, and cut to a uniform shape
2 teaspoons butter
Salt and pepper, to taste
1 teaspoon chopped fresh thyme

## Brown Butter

1 fresh lemon, cut in half
4 tablespoons butter
Salt and pepper, to taste

## Trout

4 trout, boned and filleted
Salt and pepper, to taste
$1/2$ cup all-purpose flour
2 tablespoons vegetable oil

**Potatoes:** Preheat oven to 375 degrees.

Slice the potatoes very thin and place in a large bowl. Season with salt and pepper then add the thyme, rosemary, butter, and oil. Toss and mix thoroughly. Arrange the potatoes in a shallow 8 x 8-inch casserole dish or small baking pan so that they are layered to no more than an inch thick. Bake for approximately 1 hour or until cooked soft with a brown top. Keep hot until serving time.

**Parsnips:** Sauté parsnips in a hot sauté pan with the butter. Season with salt and pepper then add the thyme. Cook until tender and some color has been attained on the surface. Keep hot until serving time.

**Brown Butter Sauce:** Squeeze the juice from both halves of the lemon into a small saucepan then drop the squeezed halves in the pan, too. Add the butter then heat over moderately high heat. The butter with begin to froth then it will "break" and the butter solids will begin to brown on the bottom of the pan. When the browning of the solids occurs, remove from the heat, stir with a wooden spoon, and season with salt and pepper. Keep hot until serving time.

**Trout:** Lay your trout fillets out flat on a piece of plastic wrap. Season lightly on both sides with salt and pepper. Then lightly coat each fillet on both sides with the flour. Preheat the oil in a large skillet over moderately high heat. Carefully add the fillets, one at a time, with the skin side down. Cook for approximately 2–3 minutes, or until the skin begins to brown and the edges of the fillets start to turn white. Use a spatula to carefully flip each fillet, and continue cooking for approximately another 1–2 minutes. When the fillets are fully cooked, the meat will be white all the way through. Keep hot until serving time.

I recommend cooking each item in the order that they are listed above. The potatoes will hold very well, and the parsnips and sauce will hold much better than the fish will. When you are ready to plate, cut a portion of the potatoes and place on each plate. Then use a spoon to portion the parsnips evenly on all 4 plates. Use the spatula to arrange the trout onto each plate on top of the potatoes and parsnips. Use a spoon to drizzle some of the brown butter over each fillet and around the plate. Being a butter sauce, a little goes a long way in both flavor and calorie count. Serve while hot and enjoy.

*continued*

*The lemon brown butter gives a real elegance to trout cooked in a shallow pan, which is otherwise a classic camping-out dish. Lemons were more special to Adirondackers of generations gone by than they are today when we can get them at the local convenience store. Lucelia Clark, serving her boarders on the Windfall around the turn of the last century, actually grew her own lemons— occasionally—from seed she'd save from a purchased fruit. In 1915, after admiring the single lemon that grew on her little tree for a few days, she made lemonade. "It was very good," she reported in her diary on the last day of January.*

*Lucelia Clark posed outside her log house near Cranberry Lake with the lemon tree she grew from a seed in 1915. P 73448*

# Cedar-Planked Salmon

*4 servings*

 Cooking on wooden planks imparts flavor into the fish. Be sure to use wood that has not been treated with any chemicals. You want an all-natural plank. Salmon can be eaten at various stages of "doneness." I like mine done about medium; but most folks prefer their fish cooked through. Cooking the fish as one large fillet helps to keep it moist.

**1 ½ pounds boneless, skinless salmon fillet**
**Salt and pepper, to taste**
**1 tablespoon olive oil**
**1 tablespoon chopped fresh dill**
**1 teaspoon fresh lemon zest**

Preheat oven to 350 degrees. Season the salmon with salt and pepper, drizzle with oil, and rub to evenly coat. Sprinkle with dill and lemon zest.

Place the fillet on a food-grade cedar plank, put the plank in oven, and bake for 20–25 minutes. Test the salmon for doneness by breaking off a small piece. If the fish flakes off easily and the meat is opaque, it is done. Cut the fillet into 4 even portions and serve immediately.

*In 1860, Alfred Billings Street remembered a classic camp meal that you can relive with this recipe. "Mart was cooking rows of trout, pinned [to a large maple block], one row over the other, with shreds of salt pork, with a concave flake of birch bark at the bottom to receive the drippings." By the time Street visited the Adirondacks, salmon had been extirpated in the region, so he planked brook trout. His contemporaries could still remember the extraordinary salmon runs of the early nineteenth century up the Chateaugay, St. Regis, Raquette, Grass, and Oswegatchie Rivers from the St. Lawrence. Atlantic salmon also ran the Boquet, Salmon, Saranac, and Chazy Rivers from Lake Champlain in such numbers that men drove a team with a wagon into the shallows during the spring migration and used a pitchfork to spear the fish into the wagon bed, "thus obtain[ing] in a few minutes all the fish needed for consumption," wrote W. C. Watson. "Many of the salmon taken in this primitive method would reach 20 pounds in weight."*

# Poached Salmon

*4 servings*

 Poaching, in general, is a gentle process. If you cooked something like a fish fillet at a rolling boil it would break the fish apart. Bringing the liquid to a boil, then simmering for 20 minutes allows for the flavors to develop. Poaching fish yields a moist, flavorful fillet that it great served hot or cold with an endless array of accompaniments from boiled potatoes, to salads, to dill sour cream sauce.

**3 cups water**
**1 cup white wine**
**2 teaspoons kosher salt**
**1 teaspoon black pepper**
**1 bay leaf**
**1 teaspoon celery seeds**
**1 lemon**
**4 (6-ounce) boneless, skinless salmon fillets**

In a large stock pot, combine the water, wine, salt, pepper, bay leaf, and celery seeds. Cut the lemon in half, squeeze the juice from both halves into the pot, and add the lemon halves to the pot as well. Bring the mixture to a boil then reduce the heat to a simmer and cook for 20 minutes.

Add the salmon fillets to the hot liquid, making sure they are completely submerged, and cook for about 10 minutes. Check for doneness by pressing gently on one of the fillets. If it feels like it will break apart with little resistance, it is done. If it springs back when pressed, cook it a little longer. Carefully remove the fillets from the poaching liquid with a slotted spoon. Poached salmon can be served hot, or it can be chilled and served cold.

In 1869, telling potential visitors to the Adirondacks what they could expect to eat on their camping trip, W. H. H. "Adirondack" Murray included "salmon"—boiled, baked, broiled, and in a chowder. What he meant, as did others who wrote of fishing for "salmon trout," was not the pink-fleshed fish that migrates upstream from the ocean, or even landlocked salmon, but lake trout. Another visitor, Joel Tyler Headley, reported hearing of hunters catching these "noble fellows" in Raquette Lake that weighed over 30 pounds. If you're a lucky fisherman, by all means use lake trout in this recipe, or landlocked salmon, which are Atlantic salmon the Department of Environmental Conservation has been reintroducing to the region since the 1960s. Otherwise, Atlantic or Pacific salmon from the grocery will work fine.

*Paulina Brandreth was a renowned sportswoman who wrote several books about the joys of hunting and fishing. She caught this 18½ pound lake trout in Brandreth Lake in 1890. P 17823*

# Campfire Trout

*1 serving*

This is truly a "backwoods" cooking method that has been used for centuries and is still effective today. Be sure to use a "green" sapling from a hardwood tree. The moisture in a green sapling keeps it from catching fire and using hardwood as opposed to an evergreen imparts a milder flavor.

**Salt and pepper, to taste**
**1 whole trout, cleaned**
**2 strips bacon**

Sprinkle salt and pepper on the trout, inside and out. Wrap the trout from head to tail with the bacon.

Find a 3–4-foot-long hardwood sapling, about a $^1/_2$ inch at its base and with a forked end at the other. Whittle the ends of the fork to a point.

Impale the fish onto the stick. Place the fish very near an open campfire but not so close as to burn the sapling. Place the end of the stick into the ground and brace it up with a rock or two if necessary. Cooking times will vary with the size of the trout, the heat of the fire, the length of the stick, etc. As a general rule, when the bacon starts to crisp and the meat of the trout flakes away from the bone, it is done.

*Arpad G. Gerster, "Bivouac, Aluminum Pond, Sept. 12, 1896, [Guide] Joe Grenon getting supper."*

This is a recipe straight from the campfires of early Adirondack sportsmen. One such sportsman was Arpad Gerster, a New York surgeon, who liked nothing so much as living alone in the woods, traveling by canoe, and eating the catch of the day. He left detailed directions for camping and eating in his diaries, including this description from 1896. "The king of all culinary processes is the noble practice of broiling. It is cleanly, perfect as to results, and its apparatus need not be lugged, being everywhere at hand. Cut a birch shoot five feet long, leaving a good crotch at its end, the extremities of which are well sharpened. Now impale a slice of bacon, then your steak or chicken or fish, and again some bacon, firmly and securely, using a bit of string if necessary. When your potato is nearly done (20 minutes), place your meat over the clean live coals, turning frequently. Fish will be done in 6–8 minutes, a chicken and steak in 10–12 minutes, the criterion being this, that each stab with fork or knife should be followed by an abundant flow of gravy or meat juice. Then out comes your jackknife, and the convivium begins. The birds furnish table music, the green fronds overhead are the roof of your banqueting hall, and the preceding labor and inherent cheerfulness of the honest camper bring that hunger and contentment which are the most essential ingredients of an ambrosial meal."

# Adirondack Surf and Turf

*4 servings*

**4 (3-ounce) venison loin medallions**
**4 (3-ounce) boneless trout fillets**
**Salt and pepper, to taste**
**1/2 teaspoon chopped fresh thyme**
**2 tablespoons olive oil**
**1 tablespoon all-purpose flour**
**1/4 cup white wine**
**1/2 cup chicken broth**
**2 tablespoons butter**

Season the venison and trout with salt and pepper. Sprinkle the venison with thyme.

Heat a cast iron skillet over moderately high heat. Add the oil then add the venison. Sear until nicely browned, about 1 minute. Then turn and sear the other side, cooking for about another 1–2 minutes. Remove them from the pan and hold them on a plate.

Reduce the heat on the pan to medium-high. Add the trout, cooking the skin side first. Cook for about 1–2 minutes then turn and cook the other side for another 1–2 minutes. Remove them from the pan and hold them with the venison.

Add the flour to the pan. Use a whisk to move the flour around to absorb the fat in the pan. Add the wine and whisk. Add the broth and whisk again. Bring to boil then reduce heat to a simmer. Whisk in the butter. Adjust seasoning with salt and pepper. Serve the pan sauce with the venison and trout.

*Brandreth Park guides Reuben Cary (standing, left), Jack Richards (right), and their dog have helped E. A. McAlpin (seated, left) and another client find a fine take of brook trout and venison, the classic Adirondack sportsman's meal. P 895*

"I am often asked," wrote "Adirondack" Murray in 1869, "what do you have to eat up there?" His list was short, including only potatoes, venison, and trout, with pancakes and bread to fill in the corners. "If a man cannot make a pound of flesh per day on that diet, I pity him!" he remarked, in those days when a sizable girth meant prosperity and many thin people had tuberculosis. "Now imagine that you have been out for eight hours, with a cool, appetizing mountain breeze blowing in your face," he continued, "and then fancy yourself seated before your bark table in the shadow of the pines, with the water rippling at your feet; a lake dotted with islands, and walled in with mountains, before you, and such a bill of fare to select from, and then tell me if it looks like starvation?"

# Grilled Marinated Skirt Steak

*4 servings*

4 (12-ounce) portions cleaned skirt steak*
4 cloves garlic, peeled
1 lime
1 tablespoon ground cumin
3 ounces water
¼ (7-ounce) can chipotle peppers in adobo
1 liter Pepsi Cola
Olive oil
Salt and pepper, to taste

Place the steaks in a shallow 10-inch baking dish.

To make the marinade, put the garlic, juice from the lime, cumin, water, and peppers in a blender. Run on high speed for about 30 seconds, until the mixture is smooth. Pour this mixture over the steaks in the dish. Add the lime halves to the dish, along with the Pepsi Cola. Use a pair of tongs to turn the steaks around and mix up the marinade a bit. Cover with plastic wrap and allow to marinate overnight.

Remove the steaks from the marinade and pat dry. Drizzle each steak with oil then sprinkle with salt and pepper. Grill to preferred doneness. Medium rare is my recommendation. After you remove the steak from the grill, you should allow it to rest for several minutes before slicing. Be sure to slice the meat against the grain for maximum tenderness.

* To clean a skirt steak, remove the membrane from both sides of the steak by cutting off a thin strip of connective tissue from the sides. This will allow you to peel the membrane away from the flesh.

*"Beef" to a nineteenth-century Adirondack family probably meant an animal from the dairy herd that had outlived its usefulness—either a cow or a bull. On her farm near Cranberry Lake, Lucelia Clark wrote on November 25, 1913, that "H & R butchered the Prince of Riverside. Too bad that the scions of royal blood should be turned into common beef." Mrs. Clark didn't record how she treated the meat from the Prince. She certainly had some way of tenderizing the beef from old cows and bulls. It was probably long, slow cooking, rather than marinating (particularly not in Pepsi), as we do in this recipe.*

# Hunter's-Style Chicken

*4 servings*

1 (3 ½- to 4-pound) whole
   chicken, cut into 8 pieces
Salt and pepper, to taste
2 tablespoons olive oil
1 cup large diced yellow onion
1 cup large diced green bell
   pepper
6 ounces button mushrooms,
   quartered
4 cloves garlic, peeled and sliced
1 cup red wine
1 cup chicken broth
1 (28-ounce) can whole tomatoes
   in juice

*Gladys Clark LaFountain feeds chickens at Maple Grove Farm near Cranberry Lake about 1920. P 73475*

Preheat oven to 350 degrees.

Season the chicken parts with salt and pepper. Heat a large cast iron skillet over medium-high heat. Add the oil, then place half the chicken in the pan and brown on both sides. Remove the chicken from the pan and repeat the browning process with the remaining chicken. Remove the chicken and set aside.

Add the onion, bell pepper, mushrooms, and garlic to the pan. Stir and cook for 8–10 minutes. Add the chicken back to the pan. Add the wine and cook for 5–10 minutes to let the wine reduce by half. Add the broth then add the tomatoes by crushing them in your hands before placing them and the juices in the pan.

Bring to boil then shut off the burner. Cover loosely with foil and place the pan in oven for 45 minutes. The chicken is done when it is tender and ready to fall from the bone.

*Hunting in the Adirondacks is not always a sure thing, as anyone who has tried it knows. Game, big and small, move to find food and shelter, and sometimes they abandon an area altogether. Successful hunters study the habits of their prey, but even they are sometimes tricked. This dish is one for the unsuccessful hunter—it consists of thoroughly domesticated meat and vegetables.*

# Side Dishes

An abundance of side dishes and relishes makes a meal special, whether to honor company or the day. A family in Thurman had only pressed meat for the main dish at a Sunday dinner during the Depression, but it was accompanied by escalloped potatoes, escalloped corn, baked beans and pork, vegetable and macaroni salad, pickled beets, grape conserve, "chilli-sauce," biscuits and butter, three kinds of pie, two of cake (plus cupcakes and cookies), and peanut butter sandwiches in case anyone was still hungry.

# Three Sisters Succotash

*4 servings*

**4 ears fresh corn on the cob**
**I tablespoon olive oil**
**I shallot, peeled and finely chopped**
**1/2 cup heavy cream**
**I cup fresh or frozen whole lima beans**
**I medium zucchini, cut into small dice**
**I small red bell pepper, cut into small dice**
**3 leaves fresh basil, chopped**
**I tablespoon chopped fresh cilantro**
**Salt and pepper, to taste**

Husk the corn and remove all of the filaments. Grate 2 ears of the corn on a box grater, being sure to catch all of the grated corn and "milk." Cut the kernels off the remaining corn and set aside.

Heat a heavy-bottom sauté pan over medium heat. Add oil to lightly coat the bottom of the pan. Add the shallot; stir. Then add the grated corn and cook over medium heat for approximately1 minute. Stir in the cream, bring to a boil, and then reduce to a simmer. Cook until the mixture begins to thicken.

Add the lima beans, zucchini, bell pepper, and the reserved corn kernels. Cook over moderate heat until everything is hot. Add the basil and cilantro. Taste and adjust seasoning as necessary with salt and pepper. Serve immediately.

*To the Iroquois, corn, beans, and squash are the Three Sisters, special gifts of the Great Spirit. In legend, they cannot exist apart, and are guarded by DE-O-HA-KO, three spirit sisters of great beauty and unswerving fidelity who protect them from blight and solicit rain. In history, the Mohawk grew corn, beans, and squash by companion planting in great gardens outside their palisaded villages on the southern slopes of the Adirondacks. The squash spread out around the ground and kept down the weeds and conserved moisture, and the cornstalks provided support for the bean vines.*

# Spiced Winter Squash

*4 servings*

 Just about any winter squash can be roasted in this manner. Acorn and butternut are readily available and familiar to most. Cooking times may vary due to different densities of the squash.

**3 cups peeled, seeded, and large-diced acorn
    or butternut squash**
**4 teaspoons olive oil**
**¹/₂ teaspoon ground dried ginger**
**¹/₄ teaspoon ground allspice**
**¹/₄ teaspoon ground clove**
**Salt and pepper, to taste**

Preheat oven to 375 degrees.

Toss the squash with the oil to evenly coat. Sprinkle the ginger, allspice, clove, salt, and pepper over the squash. Toss again to evenly coat.

Spread the squash onto a baking sheet so it forms a single layer. Bake until fork tender and the squash starts to caramelize, about 40 minutes.

*Hard-shelled winter squash keeps fairly well in a cool place. The Mohawk kept some of their squash in bark-lined pits in the earth covered with more bark and earth, and Yankee homesteaders kept squash in their root cellars. The Indians dried squash, as well, for long-term storage and for travel. They cut the vegetables into long spirals of flesh and rind and hung the garlands in their longhouses until dry.*

# Rosemary-Roasted Carrots

*4 servings*

**3 cups peeled and large-diced carrots**
**4 teaspoons olive oil**
**I tablespoon minced shallot**
**I tablespoon chopped fresh rosemary**
**Salt and pepper, to taste**

Preheat oven to 375 degrees.

Toss the carrots in the oil to evenly coat. Add the shallot, rosemary, salt, and pepper and toss again to coat. Spread the carrots onto a baking sheet so it forms a single layer. Bake in until fork tender and the carrots start to caramelize, about 30 minutes.

*Harvest time meant lots of work for everyone on an Adirondack farm, but not everything had to be harvested at once. Carrots can stay in the ground for a while—some feel they are even sweeter that way. On the Clark farm near Cranberry Lake, November 11, 1910, it "snowed by spells all day." Lucelia Clark recorded that her husband and his help "dug & drew in the carrots in the storm & put them in the barn." No doubt they sorted the vegetables later and put them "down cellar."*

# Herbed Potato Cakes

*4 servings*

**2 large russet potatoes**
**$1/2$ teaspoon olive oil**
**Salt and pepper, to taste**
**$1/2$ teaspoon onion powder**
**$1/2$ teaspoon garlic powder**
**I teaspoon chopped fresh chives**
**I teaspoon chopped fresh thyme**
**I teaspoon chopped fresh parsley**
**2 teaspoons butter**

Preheat oven to 375 degrees.

Wash and dry the potatoes. Coat them evenly with oil and sprinkle with salt and pepper. Bake until fork tender, about 45 minutes. Allow to cool to room temperature.

Use a box grater to shred the potatoes into a large bowl. It's okay to get some of the skin into the mix. Add the onion powder, garlic powder, chives, thyme, and parsley; season with a pinch each of salt and pepper. Gently mix together to evenly incorporate.

Divide the mixture into 4 even portions. Form each portion into a ball then flatten into a cake.

Heat a medium cast iron skillet over medium heat. Add the butter and allow it to melt. Add the potato cakes and cook until golden brown, about 5 minutes. Turn the cakes over and cook the other side until golden brown, about another 5 minutes. Remove and serve while hot.

White "Irish" potatoes were the staple Adirondack vegetable. They grow well in this cool climate, and they keep all winter in a good root cellar. Daisy Dalaba Allen remembered that she and her eight siblings often ate potatoes three times a day in their Baker's Mills home during the 1930s and 1940s. "I am sorry for children who know only store-bought potatoes," she wrote. "Not just the usual rounds and ovals, but, to us, potatoes with arms and legs, even looking like animals . . . red, white, and even purple." Her father was so proud of his potato crop that he would take visitors down to the cellar to look at it, stored away in wooden bins.

*A garden near Old Forge about 1910. The man is holding a potato rake, a special tool for harvesting the tubers. P 70573*

# Roasted Pumpkin

4 servings

3 cups peeled and
  large-diced pie
  pumpkin
4 teaspoons olive oil
1 teaspoon minced
  shallot
1/2 teaspoon minced
  garlic
1/2 teaspoon chopped
  fresh rosemary
1/2 teaspoon chopped
  fresh thyme
1 tablespoon maple
  syrup
Salt and pepper, to taste

*"Cook in his kitchen," Lake Champlain area, 1895. This black man is the cook at a children's summer camp, one of the few jobs available to men of his race at the time. P 38036*

Preheat oven to 350 degrees.

In a large bowl, toss the pumpkin in the oil to evenly coat. Add the shallot, garlic, rosemary, thyme, syrup, and a pinch each of salt and pepper. Toss again to evenly coat.

Spread the pumpkin onto a baking sheet so it forms a single layer. Bake until fork tender and the pumpkin starts to caramelize, about 40 minutes.

*Try an antique version of this dish by mixing the roast pumpkin with maple sugar and corn for a popular Iroquois pudding. The Abenaki were also very fond of pumpkins and ate the blossoms as well as the fruit. The Indians and the very earliest Adirondack settlers roasted squash by burying them in the embers of their fires, but by the middle of the nineteenth century most cooks in the region had a cast iron cook stove—a vast improvement in both cooking and heating the room.*

# Maple-Glazed Root Vegetables

*4 servings*

**1 cup peeled and large-diced parsnips**
**½ cup large-diced turnip**
**½ cup peeled and large-diced carrot**
**1 cup peeled and large-diced golden beets**
**3 tablespoons maple syrup**
**1 tablespoon melted butter**
**½ teaspoon chopped**
   **fresh rosemary**
**Salt and pepper, to taste**

Preheat oven to 350 degrees.

Place the parsnips, turnip, carrot, and golden beets in an 8 x 8-inch glass or ceramic baking dish. Drizzle the syrup and butter over the vegetables. Sprinkle the rosemary and a pinch each of salt and pepper over the vegetables as well. Stir to incorporate.

Bake until all the vegetables are tender, about 40 minutes.

*A primitive sugar camp near North Creek about 1880. The grown man at the right is returning with sap in the buckets on his yoke; the boy and the dog have been left in charge of the arch (the fire under the boiling sap) while he was gone. P 22248*

*The Iroquois and Abenaki have boiled down maple sap since prehistoric times, although before they obtained metal kettles from the Europeans, "sugaring off" was an even more tedious business than it is today. The Indians collected the sap in wooden troughs or bark containers and then boiled it in a hollowed-out log by dropping heated stones into it. Sometimes the boiling-down process was combined with cooking; corn boiled in sap was reported to be "delicious, sweet, and a very agreeable relish." They mixed syrup into many other foods, as well. James Smith, who was captured by Indians in 1755 and spent several years living with Mohawks, reported "the way that we commonly used our sugar while encamped, was by putting it in bears fat until the fat was almost as sweet as the sugar itself, and in this we dipped our roasted venison."*

# Braised Cabbage

*4 servings*

**½ head red cabbage**
**1 small yellow onion, peeled and large diced**
**4 cloves garlic**
**1 teaspoon chopped fresh thyme**
**1 bay leaf**
**1 cup red wine**
**1 cup chicken broth**
**2 tablespoons butter**
**Salt and pepper, to taste**

Preheat oven to 375 degrees.

Cut the cabbage into 4 equal wedges. Trim off some of the core, but leave enough to hold the wedges together. Place the cabbage in an 8-inch glass or ceramic baking dish. Add the onion, garlic, thyme, bay leaf, wine, broth, butter, salt, and pepper.

Cover with aluminum foil and bake until tender, about 1 hour.

*One of the Hooper girls, daughter of mine owner Frank Hooper, helps harvest the vegetables she and her sisters planted at their home at the remote garnet mine above North River in 1913. P 50869.*

*Cabbage was common in Adirondack gardens and the homesteader's diet. It can be kept for four or five months in a root cellar, but it was often fermented into sauerkraut for storage. A specialized kraut cutter made the job of slicing the cabbage into fine ribbons easy — one in the Adirondack Museum collection has three blades recycled from a sawmill blade. The sliced cabbage was packed into a sturdy crock and tamped down firmly enough to bruise the vegetable so that the juices started to ooze out. Salt was packed between layers. Cabbage preserved this way kept for months, getting tangier the longer it sat.*

# Braised Fennel

*4 servings*

 Fennel is a wonderful plant. The bulbous portion, as used in this recipe, has a mild anise-like flavor but is sweeter and more aromatic. It can be eaten raw or cooked. The foliage, or fronds, as well as the seeds of the plant are edible.

**2 heads fresh fennel**
**I small yellow onion, peeled and large diced**
**4 cloves garlic**
**I teaspoon chopped fresh thyme**
**I bay leaf**
**¾ cup white wine**
**¾ cup chicken broth**
**2 tablespoons butter**
**Salt and pepper, to taste**

Preheat oven to 375 degrees.

Trim a thin layer off the bottom of each head of fennel. Cut off the stalks from each head about 1 inch above the bulb. The stems and fronds can be saved for other applications. Cut each head into quarters.

Place the fennel wedges into an 8-inch glass or ceramic baking dish. Add the onion, garlic, thyme, bay leaf, wine, broth, butter, salt, and pepper. Cover with aluminum foil and bake until tender, about 1 hour.

# Braised Celery

*4 servings*

**6 stalks celery, washed and trimmed**
**4 cloves garlic**
**¹/₂ teaspoon chopped fresh thyme**
**1 bay leaf**
**¹/₂ cup white wine**
**³/₄ cup chicken broth**
**2 tablespoons butter**
**Salt and pepper, to taste**

Preheat oven to 375 degrees.

Cut the celery stalks into pieces about 3 inches long. Place in an 8-inch glass or ceramic baking dish. Add the garlic, thyme, bay leaf, wine, broth, butter, salt, and pepper.

Cover with aluminum foil and bake until tender, about 45 minutes.

*Lucelia Clark (seated center with white hair), family, and friends on the porch of her home near Cranberry Lake. Mrs. Clark was an avid gardener of both vegetables and flowers. P 63460*

Celery has become one of those vegetables that we can get at any corner store and we buy it regularly to smear with peanut butter or put in soups. It is tricky to grow, however, so in the nineteenth century it was something of a status food. It even had its own tableware. It commonly was served in a special celery vase and eaten raw.

Lucelia Clark was an accomplished gardener and grew crops unusual in the Adirondacks, like the 225 celery plants she set out in 1917. Although she started many of her garden plants herself (planting the seeds in eggshells and letting them grow on the windowsills until it was warm enough outside), she purchased the young celery plants. She probably sold the celery to the Emporium Hotel in the nearby town.

# Lumberjack Potatoes

*4 servings*

**8 red bliss potatoes, parboiled until just done**
**4 strips cooked bacon**
**1 jalapeño pepper, sliced**
    **into rings**
**1/2 cup grated cheddar**
    **cheese**
**1/4 cup olive oil**
**Salt and pepper, to taste**

Preheat broiler.

Cut the potatoes into 1/4-inch-thick slices. Arrange into 4 even, semi spread out piles on a baking sheet. Break up 1 strip of bacon over each pile. Place several slices of jalapeño peppers on top and cover with cheese. Season with salt and pepper.

*"An Adirondack Cellar," 1909. Mama, who can just be seen in the background, probably has at least some potatoes in her apron. P15641*

Place under a broiler until the potatoes are hot and the cheese is melted. (This can also be achieved in a hot oven, 400 degrees for about 5 minutes.)

*This dish would satisfy the hungriest lumberjack, miner, or farmer, although he might not recognize or appreciate the hot peppers. Chile peppers were not unknown in the region, but they usually appeared on the table in a bottle of "chillie sauce," a sort of spicy catsup flavored with cinnamon and cloves in addition to unspecified "red peppers."*

*This recipe calls for boiling the potatoes specifically for the dish, but you could heat the cooked potatoes in a skillet with grease and the other ingredients—a time-honored way of serving leftover spuds.*

# Rhubarb Preserves

*makes 1 quart*

**2 1/2 pounds fresh rhubarb**
**2 cups sugar**
**2 teaspoons grated orange zest**
**1/2 cup orange juice**
**1/3 cup water**

Peel off the outer membrane of the rhubarb. Chop the rhubarb into roughly 1/2-inch pieces.

Place the rhubarb, sugar, orange zest, juice, and water in a large nonreactive saucepan. Bring to a boil then reduce heat to a simmer. Cook over medium heat for 45 minutes, stirring often. The mixture will produce some foam at first then it will subside. After the foam dissipates, the mixture will start to thicken and look glossy.

To test for doneness, you can use a candy thermometer and stop the cooking when it reaches a temperature of 220 degrees. Another way to test is to place a small spoonful of the mixture on a chilled plate and check for consistency. If the mixture sets up and is no longer runny, it is done. The consistency of jam and preserves is a personal preference. Cook a little longer if a stiffer preserve is preferred.

Cool the mixture, cover, and refrigerate for up to 3 weeks.

*Modern cooks can freeze the rhubarb and have it with other Adirondack berries like huckleberries, blackberries, or raspberries when those come into season. Lucelia Clark and other early cooks canned rhubarb so they could have it for later. The texture was lost but the taste remained.*

# Raspberry Preserves

*makes approximately 1 quart*

**4 cups crushed fresh
    raspberries**
**3 cups sugar**

Place the raspberries in a large
nonreactive saucepan. Simmer over
medium heat for about 10 minutes,
stirring often.

Add the sugar. Bring to a boil
then reduce heat slightly. Cook
over medium-high heat for 15–20
minutes, stirring often. The mixture
will produce some foam at first
then it will subside. After the foam
dissipates, the mixture will start to
thicken and look glossy.

*"The Berrie Pickers Return:" Nora
Courtney and Mary Hubbard,
1900. P 40838*

To test for doneness, you can use
a candy thermometer and stop the
cooking when it reaches a temperature of 220 degrees. Another way
to test is to place a small spoonful of the mixture on a chilled plate
and check for consistency. If the mixture sets up and is no longer
runny, it is done. The consistency of jam and preserves is a personal
preference. Cook a little longer if a stiffer preserve is preferred.

Cool the mixture, cover, and refrigerate for up to 3 weeks.

*Berries spoil quickly. The Indians, and later Adirondackers, ate as
much as they could right after picking as a special, seasonal treat,
but the rest had to be preserved. The Iroquois dried them whole in
the sun or mixed them into cornbread or sagamité (a kind of mush
that was a staple Indian dish), or pounded them into pulp and dried
them into what we would call fruit leather. Later settlers cooked them
down with sugar—white or maple—and put them up in stoneware
jars which they covered with brandy-soaked paper or wax to keep
out air and bacteria. By the late nineteenth century, glass canning
jars were affordable enough to become a staple of the pantry.*

# Sweet Potato Purée with Brown Butter and Nutmeg

*4 servings*

**3 cups peeled and large-diced sweet potatoes**
**1 quart water**
**Salt, to taste**
**2 tablespoons butter**
**¼ teaspoon ground nutmeg**
**Pepper, to taste**

Place the sweet potatoes, water, and a pinch of salt in a large saucepan. Bring to a boil, reduce to a simmer, and cook until the sweet potatoes are very soft. About 35 minutes. Drain and place the sweet potatoes in a food processor.

Melt the butter in a small pan over medium heat. Continue to cook until the butter solids turn golden brown, about 4–5 minutes. Add the brown butter, nutmeg, salt, and pepper to the sweet potatoes. Purée the mixture in the food processor until smooth. Serve while hot.

# Fresh Cranberry Relish

*makes 1 quart*

This recipe is derived from a fresh cranberry relish recipe my grandmother used to make. While pineapples and oranges wouldn't necessarily have been available in the Adirondacks in the nineteenth century, I'm certain that anyone can appreciate the natural sweetness the pineapple adds and the clean refreshing twist this relish adds to any number of meals.

**1 pound fresh cranberries**
**2 Red Delicious apples**
**2 Bosc pears**
**2 oranges**
**1/3 cup sugar**
**1 (20-ounce) can crushed pineapple, with liquid**
**1 tablespoon orange zest**

Rinse and drain the cranberries and pick out any stems or wilted berries. Cut the apples and pears into large pieces, removing and discarding the cores. Peel and cut the oranges into large pieces.

Place the cranberries, apples, pears, oranges, and sugar in a food processor and run the machine to finely chop the mixture. Place in a large bowl, adding the pineapple and zest. Mix to incorporate all the ingredients. Cover and chill in refrigerator overnight before serving.

*Cranberries flourish in many of the boggy areas of the Adirondacks, and along with other berries, nuts, maple sap, and wild game, made possible the survival of a "hunter-gatherer" lifestyle for Adirondackers well into the twentieth century. In New Russia, Bainbridge Bishop even saw cranberries as a commercial possibility, starting the first cranberry marsh in the region in the 1860s.*

# Cranberry–Apple Chutney

*makes 3–4 cups*

1 pound fresh cranberries
2 Granny Smith apples
1 cup sugar
1/2 cup light brown sugar
3/4 cup apple cider or apple juice
1/4 cup cider vinegar
3/4 cup small-diced yellow onion
1/2 cup golden raisins
1 teaspoon ground ginger
1/2 teaspoon ground cinnamon
1/8 teaspoon ground cardamom
1/8 teaspoon ground allspice
1/8 teaspoon ground clove

Wash and drain the cranberries. Pick out any stems, debris, or wilted berries; place in a large bowl and set aside. Peel and core the apples and cut into 1/4-inch dice; add to the cranberries.

In a large heavy-bottom saucepan, heat the sugar, brown sugar, apple cider, and vinegar to a boil. Cook over high heat for about 3 minutes. Add the cranberries, apples, onion, raisins, ginger, cinnamon, cardamom, allspice, and clove. Bring to a boil. Reduce heat and simmer uncovered for 25–30 minutes, stirring occasionally.

Cool, cover, and refrigerate. The chutney will keep for several weeks refrigerated.

*A.A. Low had this lovely watercolor done for labels for his cranberry preserves about 1900. 1971.170.0003A*

Pickles and chutneys are ways of preserving vegetables and fruits, but they also add relish, in the true sense of the word, to the meal. Emma Camp Meade, an Abenaki woman who ran a boarding house in Indian Lake in the early twentieth century, made something similar to this recipe which she called Crabapple Relish—it had crabapples, raisins, spices, sugar, and vinegar in it. In 1894, the grand Paul Smith's Hotel, the "St. James of the Wilderness," served chow-chow, a relish that also appears in a century-old manuscript cookbook that belonged to Ida Beldin Parker of Newcomb. Mrs. Parker used cabbage, cucumbers, onions, salt, vinegar, mustard, and pepper. Elma Moon of Thurman called her version of this relish "Bordeau Sauce" in the 1920s.

# Desserts

A classic ritual for Adirondack summer residents is to visit a local ice cream stand after dinner. In the 1960s and 1970s in Long Lake, the ritual involved not only the cone or some more lavish concoction like a Custard's Last Stand banana split (three different flavors of ice cream, a whole banana, and any or all sauces of your choice) but a trip to the town dump to watch the black bears having their dessert.

A century ago, Adirondack dinners included ice cream, too. Guests at the grand hotels also had many other choices. Typically, they finished up the meal with two courses. The penultimate course is what we would think of as dessert and consisted of ice cream, puddings, or pastries like pies, tarts, and cakes. The final course, often labeled "dessert" on the menu, consisted of nuts and fruit.

A sweet at the end of the meal was common to residents, too. The classic Adirondack dessert is pie filled with fruit or berries. And at any time of year, Adirondackers ate that great inspiration of the French Canadians, maple syrup pie.

*The dessert course at an al fresco family reunion dinner of the Conklin family, Wilmurt, about 1890. P59278*

# Fresh Berries with Maple Cream

*4 servings*

 True maple cream is a product of "sugaring" maple sap. If you have the ability to make your own or have access to a producer who makes it; it would be a fantastic substitution for the maple cream in this recipe, which is more of a glorified creamy sauce sweetened with maple syrup.

**½ cup quartered fresh strawberries**
**½ cup fresh blueberries**
**½ cup fresh raspberries**
**½ cup fresh blackberries**
**¾ cup sour cream**
**¼ cup cream cheese, softened**
**¼ cup pure maple syrup**

In a medium bowl, combine the strawberries, blueberries, raspberries, and blackberries.

In a small bowl, whisk together the sour cream, cream cheese, and maple syrup until smooth.

Place a spoonful of the maple cream into 4 serving dishes or glasses. Divide the berries evenly into the serving dishes. Spoon the remaining maple cream over the berries and serve.

*Maple cream is the luxury product of the maple sugarmaker's art. Most Adirondack families boiled their maple sap down to the crystallization stage, ending up with maple sugar. They molded it in loaves, chipping it off and pounding it to a powder as needed through the year. Taking the syrup off the fire earlier in the process gave "maple molasses," as syrup was called. Somewhere in between was a fleeting moment of perfection when you could beat the condensed sap to prevent the crystals from forming, ending up with spreadable maple cream.*

# Honey Oatmeal-Stuffed Baked Apple

*4 servings*

I like to leave the skin on the apples because it helps to keep the apples intact. Some like to eat the skin, others prefer to scoop the filling and apple out while eating. You can substitute your favorite apple for this recipe. I chose Granny Smith because they are firm and the tartness compliments the sweetened filling.

**4 large Granny Smith apples**
**1/2 cup rolled oats**
**1/4 cup honey**
**1 tablespoon dark brown sugar**
**1/4 teaspoon ground cinnamon**
**Pinch kosher salt**
**2 tablespoons butter, softened**

Preheat oven to 350 degrees.

Wash and dry the whole apples. Use an apple corer to carefully remove the core. Start from the stem and work down into the apple. Try to leave the very bottom of the apple intact as this will help keep the stuffing inside while baking. Use a vegetable peeler to peel one strip off around the top of the apple.

In a medium bowl, combine the oats, honey, brown sugar, cinnamon, salt, and butter. Stir to incorporate all the ingredients. Divide the oatmeal stuffing mixture into 4 equal portions and stuff into each of the apples.

Place the apples on a baking sheet and bake for 20 minutes. Check for doneness by inserting the tip of a paring knife into one of the apples. If the apple is tender and the knife goes in and out without much resistance, it is done. If not done, return to the oven for an additional 5–10 minutes. Remove from the oven; allow to rest for 5 minutes before serving.

Early Adirondack settlers had a sweet life, even without expensive, imported cane sugar. In addition to maple sugar and "maple molasses" (maple syrup), they had honey. Honeybees are not native to North America, but they had colonized the continent well before the first white settlers got to the Adirondacks. Many an Adirondack homestead had a bee-lining box to help them gather wild honey. This was a small, hand-held wooden box with a sliding lid and often a glass window in which the bee-hunter caught a small bunch of bees out gathering nectar. He then let them go one by one and followed them on their "beeline" straight to the hive. There he could stupefy them with smoke and take the honey—leaving some to encourage the bees to stay and make more. In the 1880s, James Wardner, proprietor of the Rainbow Lake Hotel, went beelining each summer as an activity for his guests. "This was usually an interesting experience for city people," he wrote. When he had located the hive and retrieved the honey, he would serve it to his guests in the comb on "plates" of birchbark.

*Seneca Ray Stoddard took this picture of an Adirondack beekeeper tending his hives about 1895. P 28455*

# Layered Pancake and Maple Dessert

*10–12 servings*

 Pancakes as dessert is not something that we think of often in this day and age. However, back in the day of logging camps, nothing went to waste and leftover pancakes from the morning were often re-invented into a dessert for that evening. The high level of calories from the carbohydrates, butter, and syrup were necessary to keep the lumberjacks fueled for labor.

**8 (8-inch) pancakes**
**1 cup butter**
**1 ½ cups maple syrup**

Spray the inside of a deep 8-inch round cake pan with nonstick cooking spray. Cut a piece of parchment or wax paper to fit in the bottom of the pan. Place 1 of the pancakes in the bottom of the pan.

In a small saucepan, heat the butter and syrup until all the butter is melted. Stir with a whisk to incorporate. Ladle some of the maple mixture over the pancake in the pan then place another pancake on top. Repeat the process of layering pancakes and syrup until all is used. Cover with plastic wrap and refrigerate for several hours, or overnight.

Use a butter knife to loosen the dessert from the pan by gently sliding the knife around between the two. Turn the pan over onto a large plate or serving platter and remove the parchment paper. Cut into wedges and serve.

*Marjorie Merriweather Post, left, and her
daughter Dina Merrill, entertain a guest in the
lean-to at Camp Topridge in the 1960s. P 68639*

*Marjorie Merriweather Post Close Hutton purchased a modest
camp on Upper St. Regis Lake in 1920. Fifty years and two
husbands later, she had built Camp Topridge into one of the most
lavish camps in the Adirondacks, with sixty-eight buildings and
a staff of eighty-five. Mrs. Post entertained in a style befitting the
camp with floral arrangements flown in from Washington, full-
length movies, and, of course, Adirondack activities like lakeside
picnics, fishing trips, and hiking excursions. This dessert, taking
two classic Adirondack ingredients to the utmost, was a Topridge
favorite.*

# Strawberry and Rhubarb Cobbler

*4 servings*

## Cobbler Filling

¹/₂ cup sugar
2 tablespoons all-purpose flour
¹/₈ teaspoon ground cloves
1 ¹/₂ pints fresh strawberries, stems removed and quartered
1 ¹/₂ cups sliced fresh rhubarb

## Cobbler Topping

1 cup all-purpose flour
¹/₄ cup sugar
¹/₂ cup brown sugar
¹/₂ cup rolled oats
¹/₄ cup cold unsalted butter, cut into small pieces

**Cobbler Filling:** Mix the sugar, flour, and cloves in a medium bowl. Add the strawberries and rhubarb and toss gently to evenly coat. Portion into 4 ramekins or other individual-size oven-safe dishes.

**Cobbler Topping:** In a medium bowl, combine the flour, sugar, brown sugar, and oats. Add the butter to the bowl. Use a pastry cutter, or your hand, to blend the butter into the dry ingredients. The finished product will look somewhat dry and crumbly. Set aside.

Preheat oven to 300 degrees.

Place the ramekins on a baking sheet and bake for 45 minutes. Because the rhubarb is raw in this application, it needs a head start in cooking before we add the topping. After 45 minutes, the filling should be very hot and bubbling. Carefully put the topping on the filling in an even layer. Turn the heat up to 375 degrees and place back into the oven until the topping is nicely browned, about 10 minutes. Serve while hot.

Rhubarb is hardy and takes little cultivation—there's a patch that's been growing for a century in Long Lake. Rhubarb appears early in the season, and is as welcome as the "dandylions," ramps, and fiddleheads. It was known to our grandparents as "pie plant," but it is astringent and needs sweetening to taste good in pastry—or anywhere else. This recipe uses sweet berries for sweetening. Strawberries are traditional because they ripen at just about the same time in the mountains.

*Gladys Clark and a friend after a berrying expedition near Cranberry Lake, 1910. P 73501*

# Rustic Apple Tarts

*4 servings*

## Dough

2 1/2 cups all-purpose flour
1 teaspoon kosher salt
1 cup cold unsalted butter, cut into small pieces
1/4 cup ice water

## Filling

3 cups peeled and sliced Granny Smith apples
1/4 cup light brown sugar
1/4 cup sugar
1/2 teaspoon ground cinnamon
1/4 teaspoon ground nutmeg
2 tablespoons all-purpose flour
2 teaspoons butter

**Dough:** In a large bowl, combine the flour and salt and refrigerate to chill. Starting with cold ingredients will yield the flakiest crust. Cut in the butter with a pastry cutter or fork. Add the water, 1 tablespoon at a time, mixing with a fork until the mixture forms a dough. If the dough is too dry and crumbly, add an additional tablespoon of ice water until it comes together. Cover and refrigerate for at least an hour.

Cut the dough into 4 equal portions. Use a rolling pin and a small amount of flour to roll out each piece into a circle roughly 7 inches in diameter. Brush off any excess flour and place on a large baking sheet.

**Filling:** In a large bowl, toss the apples with the brown sugar, sugar, cinnamon, nutmeg, and flour. Make sure the apples are evenly coated.

Preheat oven to 425 degrees.

Divide the apple filling into 4 equal portions. Place 1 portion of the apple filling into the center of each dough circle. Decoratively arrange the apples, leaving a 3/4-inch border all the way around. Fold the border over the apples along edges, pinching edges together as necessary.

Place $\frac{1}{2}$ teaspoon of butter on top of the apples on each tart. Bake for 25–30 minutes. The tarts are done when the sides and bottom of the crust is golden brown and crispy.

*These lumber camp cooks are taking a little break before filling the pies for tonight's dinner, ca. 1920. P 67485*

*Apple pies and tarts have graced Adirondack tables for two centuries. Menus of grand hotels and great camps feature apple pie as a pastry course (dessert came afterwards), and diaries of Adirondack women record baking pies almost weekly. Pie makers of all sorts used fresh apples in the fall right off the tree and in the winter from the barrel "down cellar." When the barrel was empty, they made pies filled with reconstituted dried apples.*

*Adirondack pies contained other treats, as well, like pumpkin, lemon, loganberry, custard, apricot, blueberry, raspberry, peach, and real mincemeat (with beef or venison cooked with dried fruits, nuts, and liquor). Curiously, you don't find pies filled with meat on the menus of hotels and great camps. Chicken pies, particularly, were popular Sunday dinner dishes on farmhouse tables, and a French Canadian Christmas wouldn't be complete without tourtiére, a pie filled with ground meat, for the supper after Christmas Eve mass.*

# Honey Panna Cotta with Macerated Berries

*4 servings*

## Panna Cotta

¾ cup whole milk
2¾ teaspoons unflavored gelatin
2¼ cup heavy cream
2 tablespoons sugar
3 tablespoons honey
Pinch kosher salt
¼ teaspoon vanilla

## Macerated Berries

¼ cup fresh blueberries
¼ cup fresh blackberries
¼ cup fresh raspberries
¼ cup fresh strawberries
¼ cup sugar
½ teaspoon vanilla

**Panna Cotta:**  Place the milk in a small heavy-bottom saucepan. Sprinkle the gelatin over the milk and let stand for 5 minutes to soften. Heat over medium heat until the gelatin dissolves, about 5 minutes. Stir often and do not boil.

Add the cream, sugar, honey, and salt. Continue to cook and stir until sugar dissolves, about 3 minutes. Remove from heat. Whisk in vanilla. Allow to cool slightly. Strain into 4 serving glasses or dishes and refrigerate until set, at least 5 hours. Serve well chilled.

**Macerated Berries:**  Place the berries in a small bowl. Sprinkle the sugar evenly over the berries then add the vanilla. Toss the berries gently to evenly coat with the sugar. Cover and refrigerate while the panna cotta sets up.

Once the panna cotta has set and the berries have had time to marinate in their own juices, simply spoon a small amount of the berries and the juices over each panna cotta and serve immediately.

*A visitor to the Prospect House or some other grand hotel in the late nineteenth century might have been served a dish very similar to this, but she would have known it as "blancmange," the French-English version of this molded dessert made from cream and sugar. It might have been accompanied with a cooked berry sauce in the nineteenth century. The Italian version, panna cotta, has become popular in this country with our growing awareness of the cuisines of other cultures, and macerating the berries, rather than cooking them, is a more modern, healthful treatment.*

# Spiced Apple Fritters

*4 servings*

**Vegetable oil**
**1 cup all-purpose flour**
**1/4 cup sugar**
**1 teaspoon salt**
**1 1/2 teaspoons baking powder**
**1 teaspoon ground cinnamon**
**1/2 teaspoon ground ginger**
**1/4 teaspoon ground clove**
**1/3 cup whole milk**
**1 egg**
**1 cup finely chopped apple**
**1/2 cup powdered sugar, sifted**

Preheat at least 2 1/2 inches oil in a large heavy-bottom saucepan to 370 degrees.

Sift together the flour, sugar, salt, baking powder, cinnamon, ginger, and clove into a large bowl. Add the milk and egg. Beat until the batter is smooth. Fold in the apple.

Drop by the teaspoonful into the hot oil. Fry for about 2–3 minutes, turning halfway through. The fritters should be nicely browned when done.

Remove from oil and drain on paper towels then roll in powdered sugar while still warm. Serve immediately.

*This recipe uses oil for frying, a modern touch which reflects our concern with saturated fats. Our Adirondack ancestors had no such worries. Nutritional science hadn't isolated the dangers of fats then, and people generally led much more active lives than we do and burned off the fat. Traditionally, Adirondack cooks fried fritters in lard, the "tried-out" fat of a pig. Home butchers were connoisseurs of pig fat; different parts of the animal yielded different grades of lard.*

*Seneca Ray Stoddard, "Old Mountain Phelps at Home, 1882."*
*Orson "Old Mountain" Phelps was a famous Keene Valley guide.*
*While he reads the newspaper to his wife, she is peeling, coring,*
*and slicing apples to string on the framework against the house*
*where a black blanket concentrates the heat to help the slices dry*
*for storage. P 8138*

# Maple Ice Cream

*makes 1 gallon*

 Maple syrup is graded by color and clarity, grade A is typically a light amber color, very clear, and has a milder maple flavor. The grade B syrup called for in this recipe is darker and has a more robust maple flavor. This recipe is derived from one that my cousin Sean, a chef in his own right, came up with after his first year of making maple syrup with us in upstate New York.

**1 quart half-and-half**
**1 quart heavy cream**
**1 tablespoon vanilla**
**2 cups dark maple syrup (grade B)**
**⅔ cup sugar**
**4 egg yolks**

In a large saucepan, combine the half-and half, cream, vanilla, maple syrup, and sugar. Heat over medium-high heat to a simmer, do not allow to boil. Cook and stir until the sugar dissolves completely. Remove from the heat.

In a small bowl, whisk the egg yolks until slightly thickened. Add about a $1/2$ cup of the hot cream mixture to the egg yolks, whisking constantly. Now add the egg yolk mixture to the pan with the remaining cream mixture, whisking constantly. Heat over medium heat, stirring constantly, until the mixture thickens enough to coat the back of a spoon.

Strain the mixture through a fine sieve into a large heat-proof bowl. Place the bowl over another bowl containing an ice bath. Stir periodically to cool the custard evenly and thoroughly, about 45 minutes.

Once the custard (or ice cream base) is chilled, freeze it in an ice cream maker according to the manufacturer's instructions.

A generation ago, making ice cream was a favorite summertime ritual at many seasonal camps and cottages in the Adirondacks. It was a great way to involve the whole family; Mother (for usually it was she who was in charge of the cooking) made a custard in the kitchen by cooking sugar, eggs, and milk carefully over a double boiler, Father or one of the big boys ventured into the cool darkness of the icehouse and clamped the ice tongs onto a block of ice cut last winter by the local caretaker, and then balanced wide-legged on the end of the dock, sloshing the block up and down in the lake to rinse off the insulating sawdust. Then came the channeling of all that summertime energy of the younger folks; chipping the ice into small enough pieces to fit into the ice cream freezer, and when the chips were carefully packed with layers of salt around the central canister containing the custard, doing the hard work of cranking until the custard froze.

Ice house at Camp Nehasane, 1902. Last winter, the caretaker has stacked blocks of ice to the roof and carefully tamped insulating sawdust in between each one on all sides. P 23767

# Blueberry Buckle

*6–8 servings*

## Blueberries

1 pint fresh blueberries
1/3 cup sugar
2 tablespoons fresh lemon juice
1/2 teaspoon ground cinnamon
1/2 cup water

## Buckle Batter

3 cups all-purpose flour
1 cup sugar
1 teaspoon baking powder
1 teaspoon baking soda
1 pinch kosher salt
1 cup cold butter, cut into pieces
2 eggs
1 1/2 cups buttermilk
1 teaspoon vanilla

## Crumb Topping

1 cup sugar
1/2 cup all-purpose flour
2/3 cup melted butter

**Blueberries:** In a medium saucepan, combine the blueberries, sugar, lemon juice, cinnamon, and water. Cook over high heat to bring to a boil. Reduce heat and simmer until it starts to thicken, about 10 minutes. Stir occasionally. Remove from heat and allow to cool to room temperature.

**Buckle Batter:** In a large bowl, combine the flour, sugar, baking powder, baking soda, and salt. Cut the butter into the flour mixture using a pastry cutter or a fork.

In a medium bowl, whisk together the eggs, buttermilk, and vanilla. Pour the egg mixture into the bowl with the flour mixture. Stir with a rubber spatula until just combined. The batter will be thick and somewhat lumpy. Do not over mix.

**Crumb Topping:**  In a medium bowl, combine the sugar and flour. Pour in the butter and mix with a fork until it looks like wet sand.

Preheat oven to 350 degrees. Spray a loaf pan with nonstick cooking spray then add some flour. Shake the pan to coat all the sides with the flour.

Pour in half the buckle batter. Pour the blueberries into the pan on top of the batter. Then pour the remaining batter over the berries. Cover the top with the crumb topping.

Bake for 30 minutes. Check for doneness by inserting a toothpick into the middle of the pan. If the pick comes out with light crumbs, it is done. If the pick comes out wet, return to the oven for 5–10 minutes.

*Hardworking Adirondack families harvested food for themselves as well as to make a little cash. In 1943, when Marilyn Hathaway graduated from her small school in Lewis and prepared to move to the high school in Elizabethtown, she needed new clothes. "Getting the money was no problem," she remembers. "Wild berries were abundant and people had money to buy them." She started with wild strawberries and then moved on to raspberries, blackberries, and blueberries as the season advanced. She earned $100 from June to September, which bought her several dresses, a winter coat, several other articles of clothing, and kept her in spending money for the whole year.*

*People from the towns surrounding the Adirondacks took the train to the mountain blueberry patches and picked their winter's supply of berries. These folks are waiting for the train home from Mountain View, in the northern Adirondacks, in 1910. P1961*

# Port-Poached Pear

*4 servings*

**1 ½ cups port wine**
**1 ½ cups water**
**1 stick cinnamon**
**6 whole cloves**
**1 cup sugar**
**4 Bosc pears**
**Whipped cream, optional**

In a medium saucepan, bring the port, water, cinnamon, cloves, and sugar to a boil. Reduce heat to a simmer and cook for 25 minutes.

While the poaching liquid is cooking, peel the pears with a vegetable peeler. Add the pears to the poaching liquid. Cook over low heat 20 minutes. Check for doneness by inserting the tip of a paring knife into one of the pears. If the pear is tender and the knife goes in and out with little resistance, it is done. Remove from the heat and let stand for 10 minutes. Remove the pears from the pot and refrigerate until fully chilled. At least 3 hours.

Remove the cinnamon and cloves from the poaching liquid. Return the pan to the stove and bring to a boil. Reduce the liquid over moderately high heat until it coats the back of a spoon. Strain the liquid and cool in refrigerator. When cold, it will make a nice syrup.

Remove the core of the pears by scooping out the bottom of each pear with a melon baller. Cut each pear in half lengthwise. Plate the chilled pears. Drizzle with some of the syrup, and serve with a dollop of whipped cream, if desired.

*Adirondack diners—at least the male guests at the region's grand hotels and great camps— knew about port, but they mostly had it in glasses, not on fruit. Port, a fortified sweet wine originally from Portugal, was a classic drink consumed with the after dinner cigar, usually not in the presence of ladies.*

# White Wine-Poached Peach

*4 servings*

**4 fresh peaches**
**1 ½ cups white wine**
**1 ½ cups water**
**1 stick cinnamon**
**6 whole cloves**
**1 cup sugar**
**Whipped cream, optional**

Cut each peach in half and remove the pit. Set the peach halves aside.

In a medium saucepan, bring the wine, water, cinnamon, cloves, and sugar to a boil. Reduce to a simmer and cook over low heat for 25 minutes.

*This waiter at the Prospect House in Blue Mountain Lake is ready to serve coffee and fruit to finish up a meal, 1894. P28232*

Add the peach halves, making sure that they are all submerged. Cook over low heat until the peaches are tender, about 10 minutes. Remove from the heat and let stand for 10 minutes. Remove the peaches carefully and refrigerate to chill thoroughly, at least 2 hours.

Remove the cinnamon and cloves from the poaching liquid. Return the pan to the stove and bring to a boil. Reduce the liquid over moderately high heat until it coats the back of a spoon. Strain the liquid and cool in refrigerator. When cold, it will make a nice syrup.

Plate the chilled peaches. Drizzle with some of the syrup, and serve with a dollop of whipped cream, if desired.

*The cooks at the great camps and grand hotels of the Adirondacks set their tables with the best of all worlds—wild food from the forests, fresh food from nearby farms, and the wines of cosmopolitan society. Guests at places like the Prospect House or White Pine Camp had their choice of wines. In the course of an eight-course dinner in the 1880s, Prospect House diners had sherry, Chateau Latour Blanche, Veuve Clicquot, Roman Punch, Macon Vieux, and Brandies and Liqueurs.*

# Breads

Most modern Americans think of bread as a frame for a sandwich. We've lost sight of the function of the "staff of life" as a food in its own right. Hard-working rural laborers depended on the carbohydrates and proteins in bread and breads in all their forms: not only loaves made from wheat, rye, oat, buckwheat, or corn flour, but pancakes, cookies, cakes, and quick breads like johnnycake.

Adirondack bakers had three basic ways of leavening breadstuffs: yeast, bacteria, and chemical leavening agents. They generally chose the chemicals (now known as baking soda and baking powder) for breads made from liquid batters like panbreads, cookies, and griddle cakes. The bacterial leavening (*Clostridium perfrigens*) which results in what is commonly known as "salt-rising bread," is little used today because it is tricky, unreliable, and has a stinky-cheese smell, but it rescued many a woman who found she had lost her yeast culture and had hungry workers to feed. Yeast, a single-celled fungus, arguably does the best work of creating the durable, yet soft structure we think of when we picture a loaf of bread, but it must be kept alive and it takes time to do its work. Until at least the turn of the nineteenth century, Adirondack housewives kept yeast cultures alive in a medium that provided them food, usually grated potatoes and water or rye flour and water.

Traditional liquid yeast like this is vulnerable to colonization by undesirable bacteria—it spoils easily. In the New England tradition, an infusion of hops protected the culture, just as hops traditionally protected beer from spoilage. Hops are hardy perennials, and you can still find them growing at old home sites throughout the Adirondacks a century or more after the last loaf of bread was baked there. The yeast culture can also be protected by lactobacillus. This lactobacillus creates an acidic environment and a slightly sour taste. Several of the recipes in this section use this sourdough starter as leavening, although Adirondack bakers, like their Yankee relatives, probably used liquid yeast rather than sourdough starter.

# Ployes: Sourdough Buckwheat Pancakes

*4 servings*

**2 cups sourdough starter**
**2 eggs, beaten**
**I tablespoon vegetable oil**
**3 tablespoons sugar**
**1/2 teaspoon vanilla**
**I teaspoon salt**
**I cup buckwheat flour**
**1/2 cup all-purpose flour**
**1/2 teaspoon baking soda**
**I teaspoon ground ginger**

In a large bowl, mix the sourdough starter, eggs, oil, sugar, and vanilla together. Stir in the salt, flours, baking soda, and ginger. Mix until just combined. Adjust consistency with more flour or some water, depending upon how thick your starter is. The batter should be pourable, but not runny.

Heat a griddle to 400 degrees. Lightly grease griddle and ladle 1/4 cup of batter onto hot surface. Cook for about 3 minutes or until top is full of bubbles. Use a spatula to flip the pancake and cook the other side for an additional 2 minutes or so. Repeat with remaining batter.

Serve as you would traditional pancakes with maple syrup, or use them as a bread by folding them in half and stuffing with your favorite chicken salad or canned venison for a more traditional snack or meal.

*Dechene, Chartier, LaPlant, Bureau, Remillard—the French Canadian influence is still felt in the Adirondacks in many ways, including family names and food. French Canadians started moving into the region from Québec before the Civil War. Many of them were single men who came to work in the lumber woods. In the mid-twentieth century, French Canadian families came looking for farmland or to work in the mines. One of the most enduring culinary traditions these Québeçois brought with them is ployes, crepes made from finely ground buckwheat flour.*

# Buttery Biscuits

*makes 12 biscuits*

**2 cups all-purpose flour**
**1 tablespoon baking powder**
**1 tablespoon sugar**
**1/2 teaspoon cream of tartar**
**1/4 teaspoon salt**
**1/2 cup butter**
**3/4 cup heavy cream**

Preheat oven to 450 degrees.

In a large bowl, combine the flour, baking powder, sugar, cream of tartar, and salt. Using a fork or a pastry blender, cut the butter into the flour to form coarse crumbs. Make a well in the center of the ingredients and pour in the cream, Lightly blend with your hands, being careful to not overwork the dough.

Place dough onto a floured surface and make into a smooth ball and then roll out until about 1 inch thick. Use a round cookie cutter to cut out as many biscuits as possible. Gather the dough, reroll, and cut more biscuits. Place biscuits on a baking sheet and bake for about 10 minutes.

*On May 13, 1910, Henry Clark, a farmer near Cranberry Lake, took the butter made by his wife Lucelia and the eggs she had gathered to town to sell. He brought the butter back unsold, wrote Lucelia in her diary, as "everybody is using Oleo." This was a blow to the Clarks because they, like so many Adirondack farm families, depended on the butter and egg money to add cash to their household economy. Lucelia churned almost daily during the spring and summer when the cows were producing milk, and in 1901 reported proudly that she had made 673 pounds between March and November. In addition to selling it, she used it in baking— often, no doubt, in biscuits like these.*

# Hearty Oatmeal Rye Bread

*makes 2 loaves*

2 (¼-ounce) packages active dry yeast
3 cups warm water
¼ cup molasses
2 cups all-purpose flour
2 cups whole-wheat flour
1 tablespoon kosher salt
2 cups dark rye flour
2 cups rolled oats
Additional all-purpose flour, as needed
Vegetable oil

In a large bowl, combine the yeast, water, and molasses. Stir until dissolved. Add the all-purpose and whole-wheat flours, about 1 cup at a time, stirring well after each addition. When all of the flour has been stirred in, beat the mixture with a wooden spoon for about 10 minutes. It should be smooth and quite soft.

Cover the bowl with a towel and put in a warm place to ferment for 45 minutes. The yeast sponge should rise considerably and be rather bubbly at the end of this time. Now sprinkle salt over the sponge and fold together.

*Several of the lumberjacks in this crew near Tupper Lake hold the tools of their trade. In addition to the men with crosscut saws, note the cook on the right who has a loaf of bread on his knees. P 9397*

Add the rye flour and the oats, a little at a time, and fold them together. The dough should be quite thick. Add enough all-purpose flour to make the dough manageable and turn it onto a floured surface. Knead the dough for 15–20 minutes, until smooth and elastic. Cover again with towel and let rise until double in size, anywhere from 1 hour to 5 hours depending on the room temperature and humidity.

Lightly coat 2 loaf pans with the oil. Punch down the dough and divide into 2 equal parts. Form each into a loaf and place 1 loaf in each pan. Cover with towel and let rise until double in size, anywhere from 1 hour to 5 hours depending on the room temperature and humidity.

Preheat oven to 350 degrees.

Bake the loaves for 40–50 minutes. Every oven is different and even the daily weather can impact your bread baking. How crusty you like your bread will also determine how long you leave it in for. If you want softer, sandwich-style bread, you can brush the finished loaves with melted butter or vegetable oil while still warm.

*This substantial bread has a real taste of history. Wheat does not grow well in the Adirondacks and had to be imported from the lowlands. Adirondack bread bakers often substituted grain they did grow for some or most of the expensive wheat flour—either cornmeal, buckwheat, or, as in this case, oatmeal or rye. If you think kneading a loaf or two of this bread is a lot of work, consider the life of Beatrice LaVigne, who worked in a lumber camp near Colton between 1910 and 1915. She cooked for one hundred men, and every other day she made two hundred loaves. She and her one helper, a male "bull cook," mixed the dough in huge galvanized tubs. Mrs. LaVigne was the highest paid person in camp (and the only woman), earning $1.50 per day, half again as much as the lumberjacks.*

# Blueberry Breakfast Bread

*makes 2 loaves*

 This recipe can also be used to make muffins. Quick breads in general lend themselves nicely to being baked in either loaves or muffins. The recipe is the same, only the cooking time varies.

**3 cups all-purpose flour**
**1 cup sugar**
**1 teaspoon baking powder**
**1 teaspoon baking soda**
**1 pinch salt**
**1 cup unsalted butter**
**2 eggs, beaten**
**1 1/2 cups buttermilk**
**1 teaspoon vanilla**
**1 cup blueberries**

Preheat oven to 350 degrees and prepare 2 loaf pans with nonstick cooking spray.

In a large bowl, combine the flour, sugar, baking powder, baking soda, and salt. Cut in the butter using a pastry cutter or fork. In a medium bowl, combine the eggs, buttermilk, and vanilla.

Add the wet ingredients to the dry ingredients. Stir gently with a rubber spatula to incorporate all the ingredients. Do not over mix. The batter will be slightly lumpy. Fold in the blueberries.

Divide the batter evenly between the prepared pans. Bake for 25–35 minutes. When a toothpick inserted into the center of loaves comes out clean, the bread is done.

This bread is raised with both baking powder and baking soda. Chemical leavenings are cheap, quick, and save labor as compared to living yeast. Baking soda (sodium bicarbonate) has been available commercially since the mid-nineteenth century. It is an alkali and when you combine it with an acid like buttermilk or molasses, it produces carbon dioxide gas which raises the bread. Baking powder is even less complicated to use as it is a premixed combination of acid (cream of tartar) and alkali (baking soda). Adding moisture creates the carbon dioxide gas. Adirondack cooks could purchase baking powder by the end of the nineteenth century, but those who had a cow continued to use baking soda and buttermilk.

You can use large commercial blueberries for this recipe, but much more tasty, and more like what Adirondackers ate a century ago, are the tiny wild blueberries that appear on low bushes in late summer

# Cider Doughnuts

*makes approximately 12 doughnuts*

1 1/2 **cups apple cider**
3 1/2 **cups all-purpose flour**
1 **teaspoon active dry yeast**
2 **teaspoons ground cinnamon**
1 1/2 **teaspoons kosher salt**
5 **tablespoons unsalted butter, softened**
1 **cup sugar**
3 **large egg yolks**
2/3 **cup buttermilk, room temperature**
**Vegetable oil**
1/4 **cup cinnamon sugar**

In a medium saucepan, bring the cider to a boil. Reduce to 1/4 cup, 10–25 minutes depending on pan size and humidity. Allow to cool to room temperature. In a large bowl, combine the flour, yeast, cinnamon, and salt. Set aside.

Place the butter and sugar in the bowl of a stand mixer fitted with the paddle attachment. Cream together on medium-high speed until well combined, about 3 minutes, scraping down the sides occasionally. Add the egg yolks and beat until smooth. Scrape down the sides. Add the reduced cider and buttermilk and beat on medium speed until combined. Stir in the flour mixture on low speed until just combined. Do not over mix.

Transfer the dough to a lightly oiled bowl, cover with plastic wrap, and let stand at room temperature until it is puffy and slightly risen, about 1 1/2 hours.

Line 2 baking sheets with parchment or waxed paper and sprinkle generously with flour. Turn the dough out onto one of them and sprinkle the top of the dough with flour. Flatten the dough with your hands until it is about 1/2 inch thick, sprinkling on more flour if necessary to prevent sticking. Place the baking sheet in the freezer until the dough is slightly stiffened, about 20 minutes.

Remove the dough from the freezer and use a 3-inch doughnut cutter to cut as many doughnut shapes as you can. Place the cut doughnuts and the doughnut holes on the second baking sheet. Re-roll and cut the scraps. Refrigerate the cut doughnuts and holes for 20–30 minutes.

Heat a deep fryer or a large deep pot with at least 3 inches of oil to 350 degrees. Line a platter or baking sheet with several layers of paper towels.

Carefully add a few doughnuts to the pot, being careful not to crowd them. Fry until golden brown on one side, about 30 seconds to 1 minute. Turn and continue to fry until golden brown on both sides, about another 30 seconds to 1 minute. Drain the cooked doughnuts on the paper towels and repeat the process with the remaining doughnuts, making sure the temperature of the oil stays at a steady 350 degrees. Roll the warm doughnuts in cinnamon sugar and serve while still warm.

Nineteenth-century Adirondackers ate lots of doughnuts according to the accounts of lumber camp cooks and farm wives. Modern-day nutritionists would shudder at the habit, considering that the historic doughnuts were deep-fried in animal fat. Most Adirondackers used lard, which is the fat off a pig, but hunters used other fats, too. Bear fat reportedly makes delicate biscuits, and in 1913, Agnes Clark tried out a bucket of fat from a couple of raccoons her brother had killed, presumably to use in cooking.

# Campfire Cornbread

*8 servings*

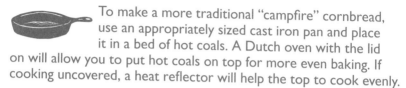 To make a more traditional "campfire" cornbread, use an appropriately sized cast iron pan and place it in a bed of hot coals. A Dutch oven with the lid on will allow you to put hot coals on top for more even baking. If cooking uncovered, a heat reflector will help the top to cook evenly.

**1 cup sour cream**
**1 large egg**
**¼ cup milk**
**2 tablespoons vegetable oil**
**1 cup all-purpose flour**
**¾ cup cornmeal**
**¼ cup sugar**
**2 teaspoons baking powder**
**½ teaspoon salt**

Preheat oven to 450 degrees and grease a 9-inch baking pan.

In a large bowl, combine the sour cream, egg, milk, and oil. Add the flour, cornmeal, sugar, baking powder, and salt. Mix gently with a rubber spatula until just moistened.

Pour the batter in the prepared pan and bake for 20 minutes. The cornbread is done when a toothpick inserted into the center comes out clean.

Alfred Billings Street, licking his chops while waiting for a camp meal in 1860, watched "a large Indian cake, arching and darkening into a rich brown," which is what you will get with this recipe with its baking powder for leavening. As far back as oral tradition can reach, the Abenaki and Iroquois have been making cornbread from ground corn and water—that's all. They used no leavening, and to modern mouths their bread would taste dry and hard. For a treat (and a complete protein), they often added beans or squash.

While it may seem more like a thick cracker than a bread to the modern palate, the Indians' plain cornmeal and water bread was adopted by white settlers and survived well into the nineteenth century. Those who wanted to take the sturdy food on a trip called it "journeycake" (corrupted to "johnnycake"); those who baked it on a slab of iron before a fire called it "hoecake." Others, like Street, named it for its main ingredient, "Indian meal," or cornmeal.

*Raquette Lake guide Jerome Wood prepares dinner for the Gerster party on Sumner Stream, 1897. P 26418*

# Maple-Glazed Cinnamon Rolls

*makes 12 rolls*

## Dough

3 ¼ teaspoons
  active dry yeast
¼ cup warm
  water
1 cup milk
½ cup shortening
⅓ cup sugar
1 ½ teaspoons salt
1 egg, beaten
4 to 5 cups all-
  purpose flour

*All ages turn out to make sugar in Keene Valley about 1880. P 411*

## Cinnamon Filling

¾ cup butter, softened
½ cup brown sugar
½ cup sugar
2 tablespoons ground cinnamon

## Maple Glaze

1 cup powdered sugar, sifted
⅔ cup maple syrup
1 tablespoon butter, softened
1 teaspoon vanilla
2 tablespoons heavy cream

**Dough:** Activate the yeast by placing it in a small bowl with the warm water for 10 minutes. Scald the milk in a small saucepan.

Place the shortening in a large bowl and pour the scalded milk over the shortening. Add sugar and the salt. Mix to incorporate. Allow to cool to room temperature.

Add the yeast mixture and the egg. Mix to incorporate. Add 4 cups of the flour, 1 at a time, mixing after each addition to form a dough. If the dough is too wet add some more flour until it makes a nice dough. Cover with a towel and let it rise for 1½ hours.

**Cinnamon Filling:**  While the dough is rising, make the cinnamon filling. In a small bowl, combine the butter, brown sugar, sugar, and cinnamon. Mix to incorporate.

**Maple Glaze:**  While the dough is rising, you can also make the maple glaze. In a medium bowl, combine the powdered sugar, maple syrup, butter, vanilla, and cream. Whisk together to form a smooth paste.

After the dough has risen, turn it out onto a floured work surface. Use a floured rolling pin to work the dough into a rectangle about 1/2 inch thick. Sprinkle the cinnamon filling evenly over the dough. Roll the dough to form a log shape.

Cut the rolled dough into 12 equal pieces. Lightly grease 2 (9 x 13-inch) baking dishes and place 6 rolls into each dish. Cover with a towel and let rise for 1 hour.

Preheat oven to 350 degrees. Place the baking dishes in the oven and bake for 15–20 minutes or until golden brown and the filling is bubbly. Allow to cool slightly. Drizzle the maple glaze evenly over the baked cinnamon rolls.

*Real maple sugar is a luxury these days, its cost keeping it in the treat category. We savor maple syrup poured over pancakes and enjoy the occasional maple ice cream cone, but it is hard to conceive of a time and a place when people used maple sugar every day. Today it is expensive because it is so labor intensive to produce, but in an economy like the Adirondacks a century ago when the family lived not on the money it spent but the labor it expended in providing for itself, maple sugar was cheap. The only capital investment necessary was a kettle or evaporator; the sap to boil down and the wood for the fire were there for the taking.*

# Dried Currant Soda Bread

*makes 1 loaf*

**3 cups all-purpose flour**
**½ cup plus 2 tablespoons sugar**
**2 teaspoons salt**
**2 teaspoons baking powder**
**½ teaspoon baking soda**
**6 tablespoons butter, chilled**
**1 cup dried currants**
**2 tablespoons orange zest**
**1¼ cups buttermilk**
**1 egg, beaten**

Preheat oven to 350 degrees and prepare a loaf pan with nonstick cooking spray.

*This cook on the Santa Clara Lumber Company's river drive in 1910 is readying his reflector oven for baking—very likely for biscuits or soda bread. P 21899*

In a large bowl, combine the flour, sugar, salt, baking powder, and baking soda. Mix to incorporate. Cut in the butter with a pastry cutter or fork. Add the currants and orange zest and mix to incorporate. Add the buttermilk and egg; mix and form a dough.

Knead the dough for about 5 minutes, using additional flour as necessary to prevent sticking. Form the dough into a rough loaf shape. Place the dough in the prepared pan. Press it gently to cover the pan evenly. Score the top with a paring knife by making 3–5 shallow diagonal cuts. Bake for about 1 hour.

*Some of the Irish immigrants who came to this country looking for a better life in the mid-nineteenth century ventured into the Adirondack wilderness. As they did elsewhere, they tended to settle together in groups. A part of Olmstedville is still known as Irishtown, and in the cemetery of tiny St. Mary's church you can read Gaelic on some of the headstones. No doubt women baked soda bread in Irishtown. The leavening is bicarbonate of soda which reacts with the buttermilk to produce the carbon dioxide to raise the loaf.*

# Cranberry Quick Bread

*makes 2 loaves*

**3 cups all-purpose flour**
**1 cup sugar**
**1 teaspoon baking powder**
**1 teaspoon baking soda**
**1 pinch salt**
**1 cup unsalted butter**
**2 eggs, beaten**
**1½ cups buttermilk**
**1 teaspoon vanilla**
**1 cup sweetened dried cranberries**

Preheat oven to 350 degrees. Prepare 2 loaf pans with a light spraying of nonstick cooking spray.

In a large bowl, combine the flour, sugar, baking powder, baking soda, and salt. Cut in the butter using a pastry cutter or fork.

In a medium bowl, combine the eggs, buttermilk, and vanilla. Add the wet ingredients to the dry ingredients. Stir gently with a rubber spatula to incorporate all the ingredients. Do not over mix. The batter will be slightly lumpy. Fold in the cranberries.

Divide the batter evenly between the 2 prepared pans and bake for 25–35 minutes. When a toothpick inserted into the center of loaves comes out clean, the bread is done.

*You can use the plump commercial cranberries that have become a staple of the Thanksgiving table for this bread, or you can pull on your Wellies and explore the margins of your favorite lake or stream. Adirondack foragers have been eating the tiny cranberries that grow in Adirondack wetlands since the days of the Iroquois and Algonquin. One Adirondack entrepreneur, Bainbridge Bishop, even tried to grow them commercially on his land near Elizabethtown in the late nineteenth century. Like most Adirondack farmers who tried to go commercial, he didn't make his fortune. He had to use up too much of his profit in getting the berries to market.*

# Homemade Dinner Rolls

*makes approximately 36 rolls*

**2 tablespoons active dry yeast**
**2 tablespoons sugar**
**1 cup lukewarm water**
**3 cups high-gluten bread flour**
**3 teaspoons kosher salt**

Place the yeast and sugar in the bowl of your mixer, and stir it around a little with your hand. This combines the sugar with the yeast, which prevents caking when you add the water.

Put the bowl on your mixer and attach the dough hook. Start on a medium-low speed then add the water. Let this mix on its own for 3–4 minutes to allow the yeast to become active.

With the mixer running, add the flour then add the salt. Allow to mix for 15 minutes. Depending on the weather (temperature and humidity) you may have to add additional flour or water. The dough should make a soft and pliable ball when finished. (The perfect dough while mixing will have the main ball of dough in the bottom of the mixing bowl and a separate smaller ball will start to detach and work its way up the dough hook.)Shut the mixer off and cover the bowl with plastic wrap. Leave it this way until it doubles in size, anywhere from 1 hour to 5 hours, or longer, depending on the room temperature and humidity.

When the dough is double in size, remove the plastic wrap and turn the mixer on for 30 seconds or so to knock the dough down. Turn the dough out onto a floured work surface. Dust lightly with flour on top and cover again with plastic wrap. Allow the dough to double in size again, anywhere from 1 hour to 5 hours, or longer, depending on the room temperature and humidity. This double proofing is what gives the rolls their unique flavor and texture.

Once the dough is double in size again, remove the plastic wrap and knock the dough down again. This time use your hands and fingers to do the work and get the dough into a rough rectangular shape. Use a floured rolling pin to roll the dough out evenly until it is about 1 inch thick.

Preheat oven to 400 degrees.

Use a dough knife (pastry knife or bench scraper as it is also known), to cut the dough into 1¹/₂-inch-wide strips. Cut each strip on the bias into pieces about 1¹/₂-inches long. Roll the cut side of each dinner roll in the flour on your workspace then place them about an inch apart on a baking sheet dusted with cornmeal or semolina flour.

Bake for 3–4 minutes then rotate the pan and bake for approximately another 3–4 minutes. When done, the rolls will be slightly browned. Remove from the oven and allow to cool to room temperature or eat while still warm. Leftover rolls can be stored for up to 2 days in ziplock bags.

*The double proofing in this recipe harks back to traditional breadmaking. It may seem to take a long time for modern cooks, even with the use of instant yeast, but the process is considerably faster than baking bread leavened by traditional liquid yeast or sourdough, which could go on for ten hours or more depending on the warmth of the house. Consider, however, that the actual work involved isn't much—you mix and let it rise, you knead, and let it rise . . . it's discontinuous work that fits in well with other jobs around the house. An Adirondack farm wife could clean, sew, or cook other dishes in the intervals, or even take a rest and read a book. On September 19, 1898, Cranberry Lake farm wife Lucelia Clark "sat up til nine o'clock baking bread and finished my book, Done in the Eagles Nest." She pronounced it "splendid" as was, no doubt, her bread.*

# Beverages

As this book is written, a new era of alcoholic beverage production is dawning in the Adirondacks. You can drink locally-brewed beer from any one of several micro-breweries, or imbibe vodka distilled from potatoes grown in Gabriels and filtered through the pure quartz crystals known as Herkimer diamonds.

"Drinking local" has a long tradition within the park. Yankee settlers brought with them the custom of brewing beer and making hard cider. Farmers grew barley and farm wives planted hops. You can still find hops growing wild around century-old home sites. This beer was still (not fizzy), and only mildly alcoholic, but a modern beer drinker would recognize it. Adirondackers brewed other beers, as well, beyond the English-style grain-based brew. All they really needed to make beer was yeast, water, and a source of sugar, and they found the latter in maple sap and molasses.

Hard liquor and wine also have an Adirondack history, but more in the drinking than in the making. Patrons at great camps and grand hotels expected the same drinks they had at comparable places elsewhere, and establishments like the Prospect House on Blue Mountain Lake or Paul Smith's Hotel in the St. Regis area kept cellars stocked with Champagnes, clarets, white wines, burgundies, Rhine and Moselle wines, sherries, ports, cordials, brandies, rums, whiskeys, and gin. Later, during Prohibition, some liquor no doubt "fell off the back of the trucks" carrying it through this wild area on its way from Canada to speakeasies in Saratoga Springs and New York City. Other Adirondack drinkers made their own. One such moonshiner near Piseco, a taxidermist by trade, advertised his "tea parties" by placing an old hat on the head of a stuffed bear cub in his shop window. Clyde Burris operated two stills in the Lake Pleasant area, and also made blackberry, dandelion, and "Tokay" wine (from potatoes and raisins), as well as beer, all fermented with Fleischman's baking yeast.

Except for that flurry of brewing and distilling during Prohibition, home production declined in the last half of the nineteenth century because of the availability of commercial brews shipped in by rail. Another damper on drinking was the influence of the Wesleyans, Methodists, and the rest of the contemporary teetotal movement.

*A. F. Tait, "A Good Time Coming," 1862. These gentlemen sportsmen are indeed fixed for a good time—there's a dog and a guide for each "sport" (both are essential in supplying the camp with venison), there's fresh trout on the way, and the camp is well supplied with alcoholic beverages. The standing gentleman is pouring himself a tin cup of port from the case in the lower left-hand corner of the painting. 63.37.1*

# Apple Cider and Applejack

A century ago, "cider" meant what we think of today as "hard cider." If you've ever left a gallon of unpasteurized apple cider out on the counter, you know that it gets fizzy within a couple of days. Wild yeast have moved in and begun to do what they do: consuming the sugar in the cider, reproducing, and creating alcohol and carbon dioxide as waste products. Our forebears expected and encouraged this to happen. For example, Julia Baker Kellogg, who lived on an isolated farm near Minerva, took apples to a local cider mill every October in the 1870s and 1880s. She put the barrels of apple juice into her root cellar, where wild yeast turned the sugar into alcohol. The Kelloggs drank this cider, and if they caught the hard cider at a reasonably alcoholic concentration and wanted some harder stuff, they could put it outside in the coldest weather. Only the water would freeze, leaving the alcohol. This was applejack.

# Maple Beer

The sugar in maple sap that is sought after for syrup can also feed yeast, and maple sap, like apple juice, will ferment if yeast gets into it. Making maple beer is simple—you just boil the sap partway down to concentrate the sugar (only half or three-quarters to the point at which it becomes syrup), and introduce yeast or let wild yeast colonize the liquid. Some old recipes specify setting the barrel containing the fermenting sap out in the spring sun to speed the process. Most suggest adding hops or spruce tips, both of which inhibit the growth of undesirable bacteria.

Sugaring in the southwestern Adirondacks in 1965 was still very traditional work. These workers gathered the sap by hand but had a tractor instead of a horse to haul it to the sugar house. P 8022

# Spruce Beer

In 1795, a French surveyor in the western Adirondacks reported drinking "*bierre de spruce . . . spoken of highly by [explorer Captain James] Cook and Americans but having in my opinion a very disagreeable taste.*" Many modern beer drinkers would agree, although spruce beer has fans in Canada where it is still brewed commercially. Captain Cook favored spruce beer because he felt it had enough vitamin C in it to be effective against scurvy. Our Frenchman recorded how it was made: "*For a barrel of 32 gallons, one boils in a large kettle twelve pounds of spruce branches. This decoction is poured into the barrel: after mixing in a gallon of molasses, the barrel is filled with cold water; the whole mixture is then stirred with a stick.*" The Frenchman either neglected to mention the yeast that got the whole thing working, or the brewer relied on his "decoction" being colonized by wild yeast. The procedure still works today; connoisseurs suggest using the new tips of black spruce gathered in the spring.

*Tupper Lake, like Riverside and several other towns on the railroad line in the early twentieth century, had a bottling works which transferred beer from barrels into bottles for sale to individual customers. Some of the barrels found their way into local taverns. In Tupper Lake it was Pabst (pictured here); in Riverside it was Yuengling. P 21784*

# Mountain Ash Cocktail

In the late 1900s, a Mountain Ash Cocktail was "the usual precursor of the morning meal at Bisby Lodge," a private hunting and fishing club in the southwestern Adirondacks. It is made by scraping a little of the tender inner bark of the American Mountain Ash into a cup, bruising it, covering it with several ounces of unblended rye whiskey, adding a little sugar, and letting it steep, and then serving it up with an equal amount of cold spring water in a tin cup.

"Before breakfast the cocktail was placed before each man," remembered one Bisby guest in 1890. "Camping out was not the luxury in those days that modern civilization has made it. A bed of boughs in a log hut close by the lake side was regarded as the height of comfort. The cocktail was supposed to overcome and banish the chill that sometimes accompanied sleep under these circumstances."

*This is the clubhouse on Bisby Lake where members ate breakfast—and drank their Mountain Ash Cocktails—about 1930. P 38122*

# Maple Rum

*Since rum is made from molasses, it seems natural that someone should have tried to make it from "maple molasses," or maple syrup. Perhaps the necessary capital investment of a still kept maple rum from becoming common. Bainbridge Bishop, whose grandparents had settled in Essex County's New Russia in 1793, was a farmer, boat builder, hunter, fisherman, and inventor of the "color organ." One of his many projects was to establish a commercial distillery for maple rum, but nothing remains of it beyond a mention in a local history.*

*Nelson Patnode was a border patrolman who covered the northern edge of the Adirondacks during Prohibition. Here he poses with a haul of illegal liquor in 1927. P 68421*

# Coffee

In the 1940s, 20-year-old Hilda Waite married a lumberjack and went into a small jobbing camp to cook for the eight men who lived there during the season. Liquor was banned in camp because of its tendency to magnify the disagreements that often crop up in a group living closely together, so the men drank water and coffee—lots of coffee. Mrs. Waite made it by throwing the grounds into a big kettle of water and boiling them. She strained the mixture through a fine sieve to serve.

*The cook in this small logging camp stands ready to serve coffee to the lumberjacks as soon as they join her family for the meal. P 18421*

# Tea

*"Charlie made a kettle full of strong tea, black as your hat, which was served to us in tin basins as black as the tea," wrote Joel Tyler Headley in 1875. He and his guides and companions were halfway between the Bog River and Little Tupper Lake, a nearly four-mile trip that today involves ten "carries," (portages). "These backwoodsmen, when on a hard tramp, do not want liquor but tea, and one who has not tried it when completely fagged out in the woods, has not the faintest conception of its invigorating properties. I took three brimming pint basins full, as strong enough, as the old women say, "to bear up an egg." At home it would have completely upset me, but here, on the contrary, it set me up, so that when we were ready to start, I was as fresh as ever."*

*A good fire in camp dries socks and brews tea—both necessary for a long tramp in 1910, or now. P 27651*

# Water

Fresh, natural spring water was a marketable Adirondack commodity in the days when clean drinking water was not taken for granted among "city folk." Hotels advertised the quality of their drinking water in their attempts to attract patrons. In the late 1890s, the Childwold Park Hotel on Massawepie Lake proudly included in their prospectus the opinion of the president of the New York City Board of Health that their Crystal Spring Water was of good quality, complete with chemical analysis listing chlorides, phosphates, nitrites, nitrates, ammonia, and nitrogen. The Crystal Spring itself was located across the lake from the hotel and the water was piped into the building. Entrepreneur A.A. Low had several springs on his 46,000 acres near Tupper Lake, and he exported "Virgin Forest Spring Water" in specially blown glass bottles via his own railroad line.

Plain "Trout Lake" was renamed "Lake Ozonia" to call attention to the purifying ozone supposedly exhaled by the surrounding forests. In the 1890s, Harvey Cutting bottled water from the spring at Lake Ozonia, advertising it as "the world's most hygienic water."

# Index

**Hallie Bond** is an independent historian with degrees from the University of Colorado, the University of York, and the University of Delaware. She was on the staff of the Adirondack Museum in Blue Mountain Lake, New York, for nearly thirty years and is the author of *Boats and Boating in the Adirondacks* and *A Paradise for Boys and Girls: Children's Camps in the Adirondacks*. She lives in Long Lake, New York.

**Stephen Topper** has a degree in culinary arts from Johnson and Wales University and has worked as a chef in several of the finest restaurants in the Adirondack region. He grew up on a small farm helping to raise food for his family and is currently an avid outdoorsman who takes pride in hunting, fishing, and trapping from the resources available in rural New York.

# Metric Conversion Chart

| Volume Measurements | | Weight Measurements | | Temperature Conversion | |
|---|---|---|---|---|---|
| U.S. | Metric | U.S. | Metric | Fahrenheit | Celsius |
| 1 teaspoon | 5 ml | $^1/_2$ ounce | 15 g | 250 | 120 |
| 1 tablespoon | 15 ml | 1 ounce | 30 g | 300 | 150 |
| $^1/_4$ cup | 60 ml | 3 ounces | 90 g | 325 | 160 |
| $^1/_3$ cup | 75 ml | 4 ounces | 115 g | 350 | 180 |
| $^1/_2$ cup | 125 ml | 8 ounces | 225 g | 375 | 190 |
| $^2/_3$ cup | 150 ml | 12 ounces | 350 g | 400 | 200 |
| $^3/_4$ cup | 175 ml | 1 pound | 450 g | 425 | 220 |
| 1 cup | 250 ml | $2^1/_4$ pounds | 1 kg | 450 | 230 |